COMPUTER CODING
PYTHON®
Projects

FOR KIDS

 **Kirklees**
COUNCIL

Library and Information Centres
Red Doles Lane
Huddersfield, West Yorkshire
HD2 1YF

This book should be returned on or before the latest date stamped below.
Fines are charged if the item is late.

29/6/18		
25/7/18		

You may renew this loan for a further period by phone, personal visit or at
www.kirklees.gov.uk/libraries, provided that the book is not required by
another reader.

NO MORE THAN THREE RENEWALS ARE PERMITTED

COMPUTER CODING
PYTHON®
Projects
FOR KIDS

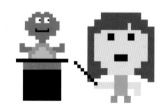

FOREWORD BY CAROL VORDERMAN

DK UK

Senior editors Ben Morgan, Steve Setford
Senior art editor Peter Radcliffe
Consultant editor Craig Steele
Jacket design development manager Sophia MTT
Jacket editor Claire Gell
Producer, pre-production Robert Dunn, Nadine King
Producer Anna Vallarino
Managing editor Lisa Gillespie
Managing art editor Owen Peyton Jones
Publisher Andrew Macintyre
Associate publishing director Liz Wheeler
Art director Karen Self
Design director Phil Ormerod
Publishing director Jonathan Metcalf

DK INDIA

Project editor Suefa Lee
Art editor Sanjay Chauhan
Assistant editor Isha Sharma
Assistant art editors Yashashvi Choudhary,
Simar Dhamija, Sonakshi Singh
Jacket designer Juhi Sheth
Jackets editorial coordinator Priyanka Sharma
Managing jackets editor Sreshtha Bhattacharya
DTP designer Sachin Gupta
Senior DTP designer Harish Aggarwal
Senior managing editor Rohan Sinha
Deputy managing art editor Anjana Nair
Pre-production manager Balwant Singh

First published in Great Britain in 2017
by Dorling Kindersley Limited
80 Strand, London WC2R 0RL

Copyright © 2017 Dorling Kindersley Limited
A Penguin Random House Company
2 4 6 8 10 9 7 5 3 1
001 – 299420 – June/2017

A CIP catalogue record for this book
is available from the British Library.
ISBN: 978-0-2412-8686-9

Printed in China

A WORLD OF IDEAS:
SEE ALL THERE IS TO KNOW

www.dk.com

CAROL VORDERMAN MBE is one of Britain's best-loved TV presenters and is renowned for her mathematical skills. She has hosted numerous TV shows on science and technology, from *Tomorrow's World* to *How 2*, and was co-host of Channel 4's *Countdown* for 26 years. A Cambridge University engineering graduate, she has a passion for communicating science and technology and has a keen interest in coding.

CRAIG STEELE is a specialist in Computing Science education. He is Project Manager for CoderDojo Scotland, which runs free coding clubs for young people. Craig has previously worked for the Raspberry Pi Foundation, Glasgow Science Centre, and the BBC micro:bit project. Craig's first computer was a ZX Spectrum.

DR CLAIRE QUIGLEY studied Computing Science at Glasgow University, where she obtained a BSc and PhD. She has worked in the Computer Laboratory at Cambridge University and Glasgow Science Centre, and is currently working on a project to develop a music and technology resource for primary schools in Edinburgh. She is a mentor at CoderDojo Scotland.

DR MARTIN GOODFELLOW has a PhD in computer science and experience of teaching coding up to university level. He has developed educational content and workshops for CoderDojo Scotland, Skills Development Scotland, Glasgow Life, and Highlands and Islands Enterprises, and has consulted on digital content for the BBC. He is currently the Scottish Ambassador for National Coding Week.

DANIEL McCAFFERTY holds a degree in Computer Science from the University of Strathclyde. He has worked as a software engineer for companies big and small in industries from banking to broadcasting. Daniel lives in Glasgow with his wife and daughter and when not teaching young people to code, he enjoys cycling and spending time with family.

DR JON WOODCOCK studied physics at Oxford University and computational astrophysics at the University of London. An avid coder since the age of eight, he has programmed all kinds of computers from single-chip microcontrollers to world-class supercomputers. He is author of DK's bestselling *Computer Coding Games for Kids* and has written or contributed to six other DK coding books.

Contents

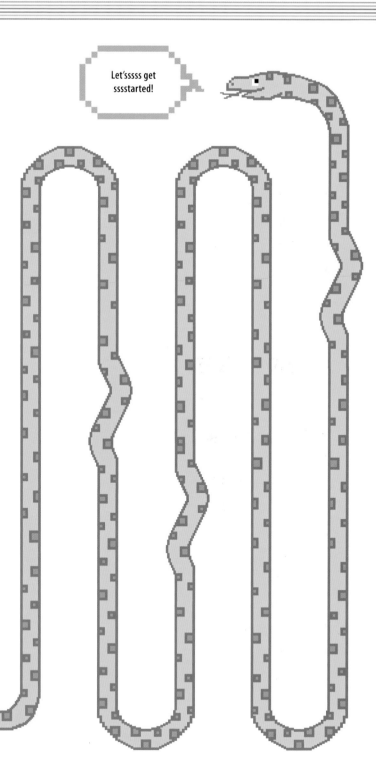

Let'ssss get sssstarted!

5   GAMES IN PYTHON

6   REFERENCE

Find out more at:
www.dk.com/computercoding

Foreword

We live in a digital world, and computers are part of almost everything we do. Not so long ago, computers were bulky, noisy machines that lived mainly on desks, but now they are tiny, silent devices hidden inside our phones, cars, TVs, and even watches. We use them to work, play games, watch films, go shopping, and keep in touch with our friends and family.

Today's computers are so simple to use that anyone can operate them. But not so many people know how to write the code that makes them work. Becoming a coder allows you to look under the bonnet and see how a computer really works. With a bit of practice, you can build your own apps, write your own games, or just tinker with other people's programs and customize your own ingenious creations.

As well as being an addictive hobby, coding is a skill that's in huge demand all over the world. Learn how to code and it will set you in good stead wherever your life leads, whether you're interested in science, art, music, sport, or business.

Today, there are hundreds of coding languages you can learn, from simple, drag-and-drop languages like Scratch™ to web-programming languages like JavaScript®. This book is based on Python®, one of the world's most widely used coding languages. Equally popular with students and professionals, Python is easy to pick up yet powerful and versatile. It's a great language to learn whether you're a beginner or moving up from a simple language like Scratch.

The best way to learn to code is to get stuck in, and that's how this book is designed to work. Just follow the numbered steps and you'll be building apps, games, graphics, and puzzles in no time. Learning to code is easier if you're having fun, so we've tried to make the projects as much fun as possible.

If you're new to programming, start at the beginning and work your way through. Don't worry if you don't understand every detail – it doesn't matter. The more projects you build, the better you'll get. And don't worry if your programs don't work the first time you run them. Even the pros have to debug their work.

Once you've finished building each project, there are tips on how to tweak and adapt it. Feel free to try your own hacks. With a little bit of imagination and skill, there's no limit to what a coder can achieve.

Carol Vorderman

CAROL VORDERMAN

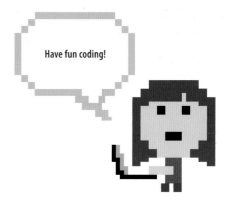

Have fun coding!

Starting
with Python

What is coding?

Computer programmers, or "coders", are people who write step-by-step instructions that can make a computer perform a task. Coders can get computers to do sums, make music, move a robot across a room, or fly a rocket to Mars.

Dumb boxes

A computer can't do anything of its own accord – it just sits there like a dumb box until it's told exactly what to do. Because computers can't think for themselves and can only do as they're told, coders have to do the thinking for them and write their instructions carefully.

△ **Performing pet**

By learning how to code, you'll be able to write your own programs and make the computer do what you want. It's a bit like having an electronic pet that you can teach to perform tricks!

Programming languages

In order to tell a computer what to do, you need to learn a programming language. Visual languages are easy for beginners to learn, while professional coders use text-based languages. This book is based on the popular text-based language Python.

Why don't you say something?

▽ **Scratch**

Scratch is a visual programming language. It's great for creating games, animations, and interactive stories. You write code in Scratch by snapping together blocks of instructions.

▽ **Python**

Python is a text-based programming language. In Python, programmers write code using words, abbreviations, numbers, and symbols. Instructions are typed in using the computer's keyboard.

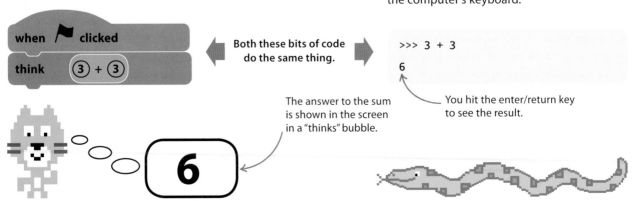

when ⚑ clicked

think   ③ + ③

Both these bits of code do the same thing.

```
>>> 3 + 3
6
```

You hit the enter/return key to see the result.

The answer to the sum is shown in the screen in a "thinks" bubble.

6

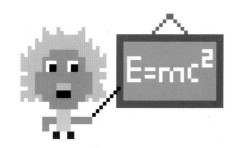

Anyone can code

To be a coder you just need to learn a few basic rules and commands, and then you can start writing programs to suit your skills and interests. If you're into science, for example, you could make an app that draws graphs from the results of your experiments. Or you could use your art skills to design an alien world for your own video game.

▽ Think logically

Coders need to think logically and carefully to write good code. If the instructions aren't quite right or the steps are in the wrong order, a program won't work properly. Think through each step and make sure things happen in a logical order – after all, you wouldn't put your trousers on before your pants, would you!

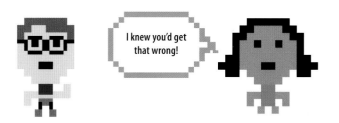

I knew you'd get that wrong!

▽ Pay attention to detail

If you're good at spot-the-difference puzzles, you'll probably be a great coder. An important skill in coding is spotting mistakes in your code. These mistakes are called bugs, and even tiny bugs can cause big problems. Eagle-eyed coders can pick out spelling mistakes and faults with the logic or order of the instructions. Debugging a program can be tricky, but learning from your mistakes is a great way to improve your coding powers.

Keep those eyes peeled!

· · · LINGO

Bugs

Bugs are errors in code that make programs behave in unexpected ways. They are so-called because early computers sometimes went wrong when insects got stuck in their circuits!

I'm on a bug hunt!

Get coding

Coding may sound daunting, but learning how to do it is easy. The secret is to get stuck in. This book is designed to teach you how to code by guiding you through simple projects. Just follow the numbered steps and you'll be creating games, apps, and digital art in no time.

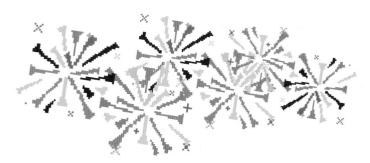

Meet Python

Python is one of the most popular computer programming languages in the world. It was first released in the 1990s and is now used to build millions of apps, games, and websites.

Why Python?

Python is a great language for getting started with computer programming. Many schools and universities use it to teach coding. Here are some of the reasons that Python's so useful.

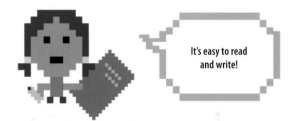

It's easy to read and write!

△ **Easy to read and write**
Python is a text-based computer programming language. You write the instructions using a mixture of English words, punctuation characters, symbols, and numbers. This makes Python code simple to read, write, and understand.

△ **Works everywhere**
Python is portable. This means you can write and run Python code on lots of different computers. The same Python code will work on PCs, Macs, Linux machines, and Raspberry Pi computers. The programs behave the same way on each machine.

▽ **Batteries included**
Programmers say Python has "batteries included". This is because it comes with everything you need to get coding straight away.

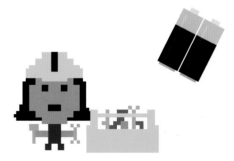

△ **Handy tools**
Python is packed with lots of useful tools and preprogrammed code that you can use in your programs. This is called the Standard Library. Using these tools makes it easier and quicker for you to build your own programs.

▷ **Great support**
Python has well-written documentation. It has a guide to getting started, a reference section for looking up what things mean, and a bunch of example code.

Python in action

Python isn't just an educational tool. It's such a powerful program it's used for many interesting and exciting tasks in business, medicine, science, and the media. It can even be used to control the lights and heating in your home.

▽ **Crawling the web**
Python is widely used on the Internet. Parts of Google's search engine are written in Python. Much of YouTube is also built using Python code.

I'm a mighty powerful program!

Don't worry, this won't hurt – much!

Python? It's a serious business!

△ **Serious business**
Python helps banks to keep track of the money in their accounts, and big store chains to set the prices of the goods they sell.

△ **Medical marvels**
Python can be used to program robots to perform tricky operations. A Python-programmed robot surgeon can work more quickly than a human one, and be more accurate and less likely to make errors.

We've been expecting you!

Action!

△ **Out of this world**
Software engineers used Python to create tools for NASA's Mission Control Centre. These tools help the crew prepare for and monitor the progress of each mission.

△ **In the movies**
Disney uses Python to automate repetitive parts of the animation process. Rather than animators carrying out the same steps over and over, they use a Python program to repeat the steps automatically. This saves work, shortening the time it takes to make a film.

Installing Python

All the projects in this book use Python 3, so make sure you download the correct version from the website. Follow the instructions that match your computer.

Python on Windows

Before you install Python 3 on a Windows PC, find out if it uses the 32-bit or 64-bit version of windows. Click "Start", right-click "Computer", and left-click "Properties". Then choose "System" if the option appears.

1 **Go to the python website**
Type the address below into your web browser to go to the Python website. Then click on "Downloads" to open the download page.

- https://www.python.org/

2 **Download Python**
Click on the latest version of Python for Windows, beginning with the number 3. The installer file will download automatically. Of the different installer options, select "executable installer".

- Python 3.6.0a4 - 2016-08-15
  - Windows x86 executable installer
  - Windows x86-64 executable installer

If you have a 32-bit version of Windows, use this installer.

If you have a 64-bit version of Windows, use this installer.

3 **Run the installer**
Double-click the installer file to install Python. Choose "install for all users" and click "next" at each prompt, without changing the default settings.

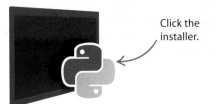

Click the installer.

4 **Open IDLE**
When the installation is finished, check that it was successful by opening the IDLE program. Go to the "Start" menu, choose "All Apps", then select "IDLE". A window like the one below should open up.

Python 3.6.0a4 Shell						
IDLE	File	Edit	Shell	Debug	Window	Help

```
Python 3.6.0a4 (v3.6.0a4:017cf260936b, Aug 15 2016, 00:45:10) [MSC v.1900 32
bit (Intel)] on win32
Type "copyright", "credits" or "license()" for more information.
>>>
```

Python on a Mac

Before you install Python 3 on a Mac, check which operating system the computer uses. Click the Apple icon in the top left of the screen and choose "About this Mac" from the drop-down menu.

1 Go to the python website

Type the address below into your web browser to go to the Python website. Then click on "Downloads" to open the download page.

> https://www.python.org/

3 Install Python

You'll find the .pkg file in the "Downloads" folder. Its icon looks like an opened parcel. Double-click it to start the installation. At the prompts, click "Continue" and then "Install" to accept the default settings.

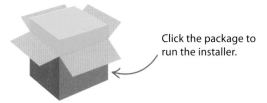

Click the package to run the installer.

4 Open IDLE

When the intallation is finished, check that it was successful by opening the IDLE program. Open the "Applications" folder, and then the "Python" folder. Double-click "IDLE" and a window like this should appear.

2 Download Python

From the downloads options, click on the latest version of Python 3 that matches your operating system. The Python.pkg file will download to your Mac automatically.

> • Python 3.6.0a4 - 2016-08-15
>   • Download macOS X 64-bit/32-bit installer

The version number might not be exactly the same as this one – just make sure you download the one that has a 3 at the beginning.

· · ■ IMPORTANT!

Ask permission

Never install Python or any other program unless you have permission to do so from the computer's owner. You may also need to ask the owner to provide an administration password during installation.

```
                    Python 3.6.0a4 Shell
IDLE    File    Edit    Shell    Debug    Window    Help

Python 3.6.0a4 (v3.6.0a4:017cf260936b, Aug 15 2016, 13:38:16)
[GCC 4.2.1 (Apple Inc. build 5666) (dot 3)] on darwin
Type "copyright", "credits" or "license()" for more information.
>>>
```

Using IDLE

IDLE has two different windows in which you can work. The editor window can be used to write and save programs, while the shell window runs Python instructions immediately.

You should come out of your shell more!

The shell window

When you open IDLE, the shell window pops up. This is the best place to get started in Python, as you don't have to create a new file first. You just type the code directly into the shell window.

▽ **Working in the shell**

The code you type can be run straight away, and any messages or "bugs" (errors) are displayed. You can use the shell window like a notepad, to test out snippets of code before you add them into a bigger program.

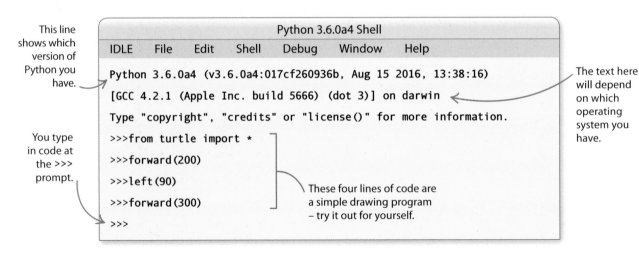

This line shows which version of Python you have.

```
Python 3.6.0a4 Shell

IDLE    File    Edit    Shell    Debug    Window    Help

Python 3.6.0a4 (v3.6.0a4:017cf260936b, Aug 15 2016, 13:38:16)
[GCC 4.2.1 (Apple Inc. build 5666) (dot 3)] on darwin
Type "copyright", "credits" or "license()" for more information.
>>>from turtle import *
>>>forward(200)
>>>left(90)
>>>forward(300)
>>>
```

You type in code at the >>> prompt.

The text here will depend on which operating system you have.

These four lines of code are a simple drawing program – try it out for yourself.

EXPERT TIPS

Different windows

To help you know which window you should type your code in, we've given each window in IDLE a different colour.

Shell window

Editor window

▽ **Give the shell a test run**

Type each of these code snippets into the shell window and press the enter/return key after each one. The first line displays a message and the second line does a calculation. Can you work out what the third line does?

```
>>> print('I am 10 years old')
```

```
>>> 123 + 456 * 7 / 8
```

```
>>> ''.join(reversed('Time to code'))
```

The editor window

The shell can't save your code, so when you close the shell window the code you typed is lost forever. That's why you should use IDLE's editor window when you work on a project. This window lets you save your code. It also has built-in tools to help you write your programs and to trouble-shoot any errors.

▽ **The editor window**
To open the editor window in IDLE, click on the File menu at the top and choose New File. An empty editor window will then appear. You'll use the editor window to write and run programs for the projects in this book.

You type the code in here. This program prints a list that tells you which numbers are even and which ones are odd.

The name of the file is shown here.

You can run your programs from this menu.

The menu bar for the editor window is different to the one for the shell.

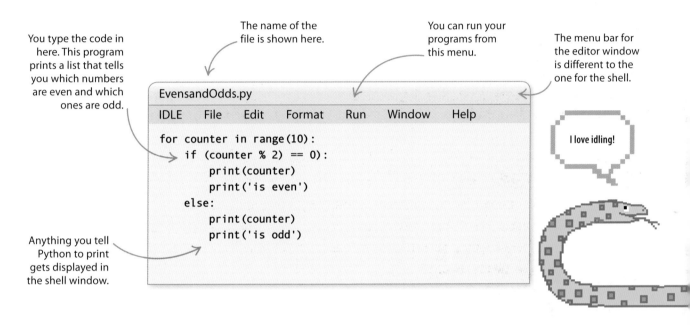

```
EvensandOdds.py

IDLE    File    Edit    Format    Run    Window    Help

for counter in range(10):
    if (counter % 2) == 0:
        print(counter)
        print('is even')
    else:
        print(counter)
        print('is odd')
```

I love idling!

Anything you tell Python to print gets displayed in the shell window.

Colours in the code

IDLE automatically colours the text to highlight different parts of the code. The colours make it easier to understand the code, and they're useful when you're trying to spot mistakes.

◁ **Symbols and names**
Most code text is coloured black.

◁ **Output**
Any text produced when a program runs is blue.

◁ **Built-in commands**
Python commands, such as `'print'`, are shown in purple.

◁ **Errors**
Python uses red to alert you to any errors in your code.

◁ **Keywords**
Certain words, such as "`if`" and "`else`", are special words that Python uses. They are called keywords and are shown in orange.

◁ **Text in quotes**
Text in quote marks is green. A green bracket around text shows you're missing a quote mark.

First
steps

Your first program

Now that you've installed Python and IDLE, it's time to write your first program in Python. Follow these steps to create a simple program that greets the user with a cheery message.

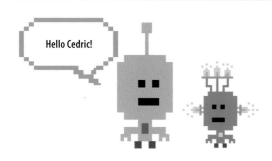

Hello Cedric!

How it works

The program first displays the message "Hello, World!" and then asks your name. Once you've typed in your name, it says hello again, but this time it includes your name in the greeting. The program uses something called a variable to remember your name. A variable is used in coding to store information.

▷ **Hello World flowchart**
Programmers use diagrams called flowcharts to plan their programs and to show how they work. Each step is shown in a box, with an arrow leading to the next step. Sometimes the steps are questions and have more than one arrow leading onwards, depending on the answer to the question.

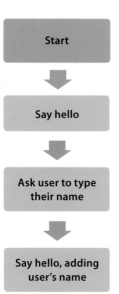

Start

Say hello

Ask user to type their name

Say hello, adding user's name

End

Hello, World!

1 **Launch IDLE**
A shell window appears when you start IDLE. Ignore it and click on File in the IDLE menu. Choose New File to create an empty editor window where you can write your program.

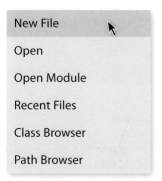

New File

Open

Open Module

Recent Files

Class Browser

Path Browser

2 **Type the first line**
In the editor window, type this line of text. The word "print" is a Python instruction that tells the computer to display something on the screen, such as the words "Hello, World!"

```
print('Hello, World!')
```

3 **Save your file**
Before you can run the code, you must save it. Go to the File menu and choose Save.

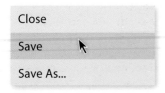

Close

Save

Save As...

4 **Save the file**
A pop-up box will appear. Type in a name for your program, such as "helloworld.py", and click Save.

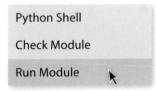

Save As: helloworld.py
Tags:
Where: Documents

Cancel   Save

Type the name of your program here.

5 **Check it works**
Now run the first line of the program to see if it works. Open the "Run" menu and choose "Run Module". You should see the message "Hello, World!" in the shell window.

Python Shell

Check Module

Run Module

```
>>>
Hello, World!
>>>
```

The message will appear in the shell.

6 **Fix mistakes**
If the code isn't working, stay calm! Every programmer makes mistakes, and finding these "bugs" is vital if you want to become an expert at coding. Go back and check your code for typing errors. Did you include the brackets? Did you spell the word "print" correctly? Fix any mistakes, then try running the code again.

. . . EXPERT TIPS

Keyboard shortcut

A handy shortcut to run a program from the editor window is simply to press F5 on your keyboard. This is a lot quicker than selecting "Run" and then "Run Module".

7 **Add more lines**
Go back to the editor window and add two more lines to your script. Now the middle line asks for your name and then stores it in a variable. The last line uses your name to print a new greeting. You can change it to a different greeting if you prefer – as polite or as rude as you like!

```
print('Hello, World!')
person = input('What's your name?')
print('Hello,', person)
```

This line asks for the user's name and stores it in a variable called "person".

8 **Final task**
Run the code again to check it. When you type in your name and hit the enter/return key, the shell should show a personalized message. Congratulations on completing your first Python program! You've taken your first steps towards becoming a powerful programmer.

```
Hello, World!
What's your name?Josh
Hello, Josh
```

User's name

Variables

If you want to write useful code, you'll need to be able to store and label pieces of information. That's what variables do. Variables are great for all sorts of things – from tracking your score in a game to performing calculations and holding lists of items.

How to create a variable

A variable needs a name. Think of a name that will remind you what's inside the variable. Then decide what you want to store in the variable. This is the variable's value. Type the name, followed by an equals sign, followed by the value. We call this "assigning a value" to the variable.

△ **Storage box**
A variable is like a box with a name label. You can store data in the box and then use the name to find the data again when you need to use it.

1 Assign a value
In the shell window, type this line of code to create the variable **age** and assign a value to it. Use your own age if you want.

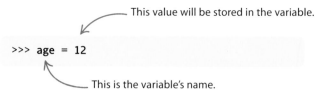

This value will be stored in the variable.

```
>>> age = 12
```

This is the variable's name.

2 Print the value
Now type the line of code shown on the right into the shell window. Hit the enter/return key to see what happens.

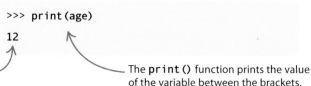

```
>>> print(age)
12
```

The value of **age**

The **print()** function prints the value of the variable between the brackets.

Naming variables

Choosing good names for your variables will make your program easier to understand. For example, a variable tracking a player's lives in a game could be called **lives_remaining**, rather than just **lives** or **lr**. Variable names can contain letters, numbers, and underscores, but they should begin with a letter. Follow the rules shown here and you won't go wrong.

Dos and don'ts
- Start the variable's name with a letter.
- Any letter or number can be used in the name.
- Symbols such as -, /, #, or @ aren't allowed.
- Spaces can't be used.
- An underscore (_) can be used instead of a space.
- Uppercase (capitals) and lowercase letters are different. Python will treat "Score" and "score" as two different variables.
- Avoid words Python uses as commands, such as "print".

Integers and floats

In coding, whole numbers are called integers, while numbers with a decimal point in them are known as floats. Programs usually count things using integers. Floats are more often used for measurements.

1 sheep (an integer)

0.5 sheep (a float)

Using numbers

Variables can be used to store numbers and do sums. You can use them with symbols to do calculations, just like you do in maths. Some of these symbols will be familiar, but watch out for the symbols meaning "multiply" and "divide" – they're slightly different from the ones you use in class.

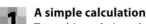

Symbol	Meaning
+	add
–	subtract
*	multiply
/	divide

Some of the Python maths symbols

Create a new variable, **x**, and give it the value 6.

1 **A simple calculation**
Type this code in a shell window. It uses numbers stored in two variables, named **x** and **y**, to carry out a simple multiplication. Hit the enter/return key to get the answer.

```
>>> x = 6
>>> y = x * 7
>>> print(y)
42
```

The result of the calculation

Print the value of **y**.

Multiply **x** by 7 and store the result in **y**.

Change the value of **x**.

2 **Change a value**
To change the value of a variable, you just assign a new value to it. In your code, change the value of **x** to 10 and run the calculation again. What do you expect the result to be?

```
>>> x = 10
>>> print(y)
42
```

The result hasn't changed – next we'll find out why.

Update the value of **y**.

3 **Update the value**
The value of **y** needs to be updated to get the correct result. Type these lines. Now the code assigns the new value to **y** after **x** has been changed. If you update the value of one variable in your own programs, always check to see if you need to update any others.

```
>>> x = 10
>>> y = x * 7
>>> print(y)
70
```

Working with strings

Coders use the word "string" for any data made up of a sequence of letters or other characters. Words and sentences are stored as strings. Almost all programs use strings at some point. Every character that you can type on your keyboard, and even those you can't, can be stored in a string.

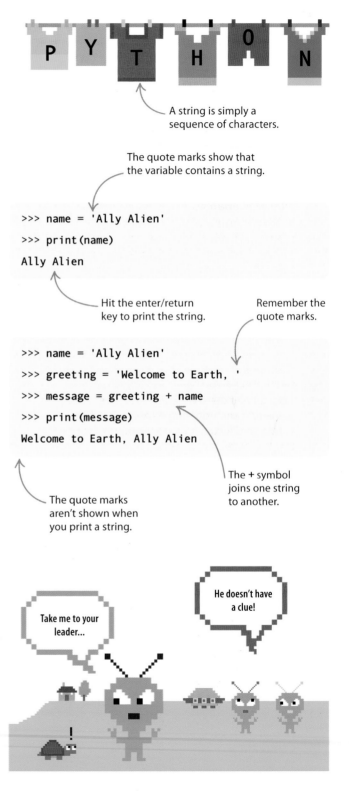

A string is simply a sequence of characters.

1 **Strings in variables**
Strings can be put into variables. Type this code into the shell window. It assigns the string **'Ally Alien'** to the variable **name** and then displays it. Strings must always have quotation marks at the beginning and end.

The quote marks show that the variable contains a string.

```
>>> name = 'Ally Alien'
>>> print(name)
Ally Alien
```

Hit the enter/return key to print the string.

2 **Combining strings**
Variables become really useful when you combine them to make new variables. If you add two strings together, you can store the combination in a new variable. Try this out.

Remember the quote marks.

```
>>> name = 'Ally Alien'
>>> greeting = 'Welcome to Earth, '
>>> message = greeting + name
>>> print(message)
Welcome to Earth, Ally Alien
```

The quote marks aren't shown when you print a string.

The + symbol joins one string to another.

⸬ ▪ ▪ EXPERT TIPS

Length of a string

You can use a handy trick, **len()**, to count the number of characters in a string (including the spaces). The command **len()** is an example of what coders call a function. (You'll use lots of functions in this book.) To find out how many characters there are in **'Welcome to Earth, Ally Alien'**, type the line below into the shell once you've created the string, then hit enter/return.

```
>>> len(message)
    28
```

The number of characters counted

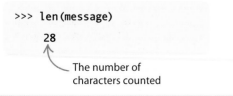

Take me to your leader...

He doesn't have a clue!

Lists

When you want to store a lot of data, or perhaps the order of the data is important, you may need to use a list. A list can hold many items together and keep them in order. Python gives each item a number that shows its position in the list. You can change the items in the list at any time.

1 **Multiple variables**
Imagine you're writing a multiplayer game and want to store the names of the players in each team. You could create a variable for each player, which might look like this...

With three players per team, you'd need six variables.

```
>>> rockets_player_1 = 'Rory'
>>> rockets_player_2 = 'Rav'
>>> rockets_player_3 = 'Rachel'
>>> planets_player_1 = 'Peter'
>>> planets_player_2 = 'Pablo'
>>> planets_player_3 = 'Polly'
```

2 **Put a list in a variable**
...but what if there were six players per team? Managing and updating so many variables would be difficult. It would be better to use a list. To create a list, you surround the items you want to store with square brackets. Try out these lists in the shell.

The list items must be separated by commas.

```
>>> rockets_players = ['Rory', 'Rav',
'Rachel', 'Renata', 'Ryan', 'Ruby']
>>> planets_players = ['Peter', 'Pablo',
'Polly', 'Penny', 'Paula', 'Patrick']
```

This list is stored in the variable `planets_players`.

This line gets the first item in the list, from position 0.

3 **Getting items from a list**
Once your data is in a list, it's easy to work with. To get an item out of a list, first type the name of the list. Then add the item's position in the list, putting it inside square brackets. Be careful: Python starts counting list items from 0 rather than 1. Now try getting different players' names out of your team lists. The first player is at position 0, while the last player is at position 5.

```
>>> rockets_players[0]
'Rory'
>>> planets_players[5]
'Patrick'
```

This line gets the last item in the list, from position 5.

Hit enter/return to retrieve the item.

Making decisions

Every day you make decisions about what to do next, based on the answers to questions you ask yourself. For example, "Is it raining?", "Have I done my homework?", "Am I a horse?" Computers also make decisions by asking questions.

Questions that compare

The questions that computers ask themselves usually involve comparing one thing with another. For example, a computer might ask if one number is bigger than another. If it is, the computer might then decide to run a block of code that would otherwise be skipped.

▷ **Boolean values**
The answers to the questions computers ask have only two possible values: True or False. Python calls these two values Boolean values, and they must always start with a capital letter. You can store a Boolean value in a variable.

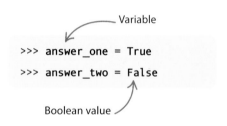

Variable

```
>>> answer_one = True
>>> answer_two = False
```

Boolean value

· · · EXPERT TIPS

Equals signs

In Python you can use a single equals sign or a double equals sign. They mean slightly different things. Use a single equals = sign when you want to set the value of a variable. Typing **age = 10**, for example, sets the value of the variable **age** to 10. Use a double equals == sign when you want to compare two values, as in the example below.

This sets the value of the variable.

```
>>> age = 10
>>> if age == 10:
        print('You are ten years old.')
```

This compares your age with the variable.

The code prints the message if the two match.

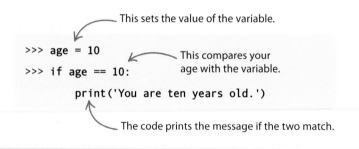

▽ **Logical operators**
These symbols tell computers to make comparisons. Programmers call them logical operators. You may have used some of them in maths. The words "and" and "or" can also be used as logical operators in computer code.

Symbol	Meaning
==	equal to
!=	not equal to
<	less than
>	greater than

Pineapples and zebras

Let's try an example using the shell. We can represent having five pineapples and two zebras by using the variables `pineapples` and `zebras`. Type these lines into the shell.

```
>>> pineapples = 5
>>> zebras = 2
```

This variable stores the number of pineapples.

This variable stores the number of zebras.

▽ ▷ Make comparisons

Now try typing the following lines of code to compare the values of the two variables. After you've typed each line, press the return key and Python will tell you if the statements are True or False.

The number of pineapples is greater than the number of zebras.

```
>>> pineapples > zebras
True
```

```
>>> zebras < pineapples
True
```

The number of zebras is less than the number of pineapples.

The number of pineapples and the number of zebras aren't equal.

```
>>> pineapples == zebras
False
```

Boolean expressions

Statements about variables and values that use the logical operators always give us a Boolean value, such as True or False. Because of this, these statements are called Boolean expressions. All of our statements about pineapples and zebras are Boolean expressions.

Variable ———   ——— Logical operator

```
>>> pineapples != zebras
True
```

Boolean value   Variable

▽ Multiple comparisons

You can use **and** and **or** to combine more than one comparison. If you use **and**, both parts of the comparison must be correct for the statement to be True. If you use **or**, only one part needs to be correct.

```
>>> (pineapples == 3) and (zebras == 2)
False
```

One part (`pineapples == 3`) is incorrect, so the statement is False.

```
>>> (pineapples == 3) or (zebras == 2)
True
```

One part is correct (`zebras == 2`), so the statement is True.

Ride the rollercoaster

A sign at the theme park says you must be over 8 years old and taller than 1.4 metres to ride the rollercoaster. Mia is 10 years old and 1.5 metres tall. Let's use the shell to check whether she can go for a ride. Type the following lines of code to create variables for Mia's age and height and assign the correct values to them. Type the rules for going on the rollercoaster as a Boolean expression, then hit the enter/return key.

You can't ride – you're too small!

But I'm 100 years old!

These two lines assign values to the variables.

```
>>> age = 10
>>> height = 1.5
>>> (age > 8) and (height > 1.4)
True
```

This is a Boolean expression meaning "older than 8 and more than 1.4 metres tall".

Mia can go on the rollercoaster!

Branching

Computers often need to make decisions about which parts of a program to run. This is because most programs are designed to do different things in different situations. The route through the program splits like a path branching off into side paths, each leading to a different place.

Condition

A condition is a Boolean expression (a True-or-False comparison) that helps a computer decide which route to take when it reaches a branch in the code.

▷ **School or park?**
Imagine you have to decide what route to walk each day based on the answer to the question "Is today a weekday?" If it's a weekday, you take the route to school; if it's not, you take the route to the park. In Python, the different routes through a program lead to different blocks of code. A block can be one statement or several, all indented by four spaces. The computer uses a test called a condition to figure out which blocks it should run next.

▷ One branch

The simplest branching command is an `if` statement. It only has one branch, which the computer takes if the condition is True. This program asks the user to say if it's dark outside. If it is, the program pretends that the computer is going to sleep! If it's not dark, `is_dark == 'y'` is False, so the "Goodnight!" message isn't displayed.

This line asks the user to reply "y" (yes) or "n" (no).

```
is_dark = input('Is it dark outside? y/n)')
if is_dark == 'y':
    print('Goodnight! Zzzzzzzzzzzzzzz....')
```

Condition

This branch is taken if the condition is True.

The code shows this message in the shell window.

▷ Two branches

Do you want a program to do one thing if a condition's True and another thing if it's False? If so, you need a command with two branches, called an `if-else` statement. This program asks if the user has tentacles. If they answer "Yes", it decides they must be an octopus! If they answer "No", it decides they're human. Each decision prints a different message.

This line asks for input from the user.

Condition

```
tentacles = input('Do you have tentacles? (n/y)')
if tentacles == 'y':
    print('I never knew octopuses could type!')
else:
    print('Greetings, human!')
```

This block runs if the condition is True.

This block runs if the condition is False.

▷ Multiple branches

When there are more than two possible paths, the statement `elif` (short for "else-if") comes in handy. This program asks the user to type in the weather forecast: either "rain", "snow", or "sun". It then chooses one of three branches and weather conditions.

```
weather = input ('What is the forecast for today? (rain/snow/sun)')

if weather == 'rain':
    print('Remember your umbrella!')
elif weather == 'snow':
    print('Remember your woolly gloves!')
else:
    print('Remember your sunglasses!')
```

First condition

This block runs if the first condition is True.

Second condition

This block runs if the second condition is True.

This block runs if both conditions are False.

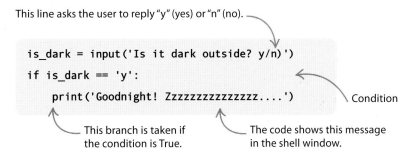

△ How it works

An `elif` statement must always come after `if` and before `else`. In this code, `elif` checks for snow only when the condition set by the `if` statement is False. You could insert additional `elif` statements to check for more types of weather.

Loopy loops

Computers are great at doing boring tasks without complaining. Programmers aren't, but they are good at getting computers to do repetitive work for them – by using loops. A loop runs the same block of code over and over again. There are several different types of loop.

For loops

When you know how many times you want to run a block of code, you can use a **for** loop. In this example, Emma has written a program to make a sign for her door. It prints "Emma's Room – Keep Out!!!" ten times. Try out her code for yourself in the shell. (After typing the code and hitting enter/return, press backspace to remove the indent and then hit enter/return again.)

This is the loop variable.

The loop runs 10 times.

```
>>> for counter in range(1, 11):
        print('Emma\'s Room - Keep Out!!!')
```

Indent the commands in the body 4 spaces.

The line that gets repeated is called the loop body.

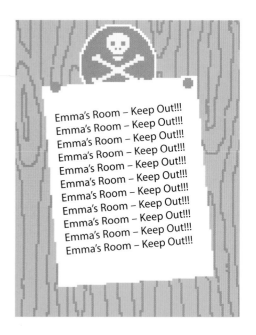

Emma's Room – Keep Out!!!
Emma's Room – Keep Out!!!
Emma's Room – Keep Out!!!
Emma's Room – Keep Out!!!
Emma's Room – Keep Out!!!
Emma's Room – Keep Out!!!
Emma's Room – Keep Out!!!
Emma's Room – Keep Out!!!
Emma's Room – Keep Out!!!
Emma's Room – Keep Out!!!

▽ **Loop variable**

The loop variable keeps track of how many times we've gone round the loop so far. The first time round it's equal to the first number in the list specified by **range(1, 11)**. The second time round it's equal to the second number in the list, and so on. When we've used all the numbers in the list, we stop looping.

First loop

Second loop

Third loop

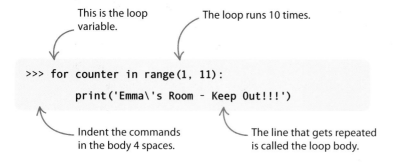

Loop variable = 1

Loop variable = 2

Loop variable = 3

■ ■ ■ **EXPERT TIPS**

Range

In Python code, the word "range" followed by two numbers within brackets stands for "all the numbers from the first number to one less than the second number". So **range(1, 4)** means the numbers 1, 2, and 3 – but not 4. In Emma's "Keep Out" program, **range(1, 11)** is the numbers 1, 2, 3, 4, 5, 6, 7, 8, 9, and 10.

Escape character (\)

The backslash in **Emma\'s Room** tells Python to ignore the apostrophe so that it doesn't treat it as the quotation mark that closes the whole string. A backslash used like this is called an escape character. It tells Python not to count the next character when working out if the line makes sense or contains errors.

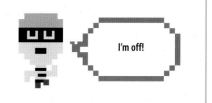

I'm off!

While loops

I can see the future, and it's completely loopy!

What happens if you don't know how many times you want to repeat the code? Do you need a crystal ball or some other way of seeing into the future? No, it's okay! You can use a **while** loop.

▷ **Loop condition**

A **while** loop doesn't have a loop variable that's set to a range of values. Instead it has a loop condition. This is a Boolean expression that can be either True or False. It's a bit like a bouncer at a disco asking you if you've got a ticket. If you have one (True), head straight for the dance floor; if you don't (False), the bouncer won't let you in. In programming, if the loop condition isn't True, you won't get into the loop!

You can't come in – your loop condition isn't true!

Disco here today!

▽ **Balancing act**

In this example, Ahmed has written a program to keep track of how many of his troupe of acrobatic hippopotamuses have balanced on top of each other to make a tower. Read through the code and see if you can figure out how it works.

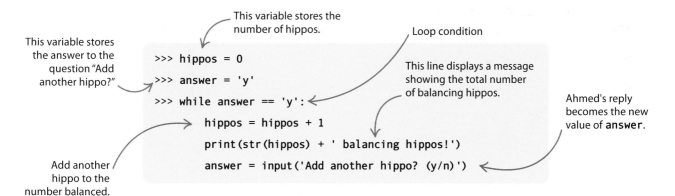

This variable stores the number of hippos.

This variable stores the answer to the question "Add another hippo?"

Loop condition

This line displays a message showing the total number of balancing hippos.

Ahmed's reply becomes the new value of **answer**.

Add another hippo to the number balanced.

```
>>> hippos = 0
>>> answer = 'y'
>>> while answer == 'y':
        hippos = hippos + 1
        print(str(hippos) + ' balancing hippos!')
        answer = input('Add another hippo? (y/n)')
```

▷ **How it works**

The loop condition in Ahmed's program is `answer == 'y'`. This means that the user wants to add a hippo. In the body of the loop we add one to the number of hippos balanced, then ask the user if they want to add another. If they answer by typing "y" (for yes), the loop condition is True so we go round the loop again. If they answer "n" (no), the loop condition is False and the program leaves the loop.

Infinite loops

Sometimes you may want a `while` loop to keep going for as long as the program is running. This kind of loop is called an infinite loop. Lots of video-game programs use an infinite loop known as a main loop.

There is no False option to escape the loop.

```
>>> while True:
        print('This is an infinite loop!')
```

△ **Into infinity**

You make an infinite loop by setting the loop condition to a constant value: True. Because this value never changes, the loop will never exit. Try this `while` loop in the shell. It has no False option, so the loop will print "This is an infinite loop!" nonstop until you quit the program.

▽ **Escaping infinity**

You can deliberately use an infinite loop to get input from the user. This (annoying) program asks if the user is bored. As long as they type "n", it keeps asking the question. If they get fed up and type "y", it tells them they're rude and uses the `break` command to leave the loop!

The True condition is that the user is not bored yet (`'n'`).

```
>>> while True:
        answer = input('Are you bored yet? (y/n)')
        if answer == 'y':
            print('How rude!')
            break
```

The False condition (`'y'`) triggers the `break` command.

EXPERT TIPS

Stopping the loop

If you don't want an infinite loop, it's important to make sure that the body of a `while` loop does something that could make the loop condition False. But don't worry – if you accidentally code an infinite loop, you can escape from it by pressing the C key while holding down the Ctrl (control) key. You may have to press Ctrl-C several times before you quit the loop.

Ctrl-C

Loops inside loops

Can the body of a loop have another loop within it? Yes! This is called a nested loop. It's like Russian dolls, where each doll fits inside a larger doll. In a nested loop, an inner loop runs inside an outer loop.

I like Russian dolls – but they're always so full of themselves!

Indent the body

The code in the body of a loop should be indented four spaces. If it isn't, Python will show an error message and the code won't run. With nested loops (one loop inside another), the body of the inner loop must be indented an extra four spaces. Python automatically indents new lines in loops, but you should always check that each line is indented by the correct number of spaces.

SyntaxError

❌ unexpected indent

OK

The loop variable of the outer loop is `hooray_counter`.

▷ **One loop inside another**

In this example, Emma has changed her "Keep Out" program into a "Three Cheers" program that prints "Hip, Hip, Hooray!" three times. Because each cheer includes the word "Hip" twice, she uses a nested loop to print it.

```
>>> for hooray_counter in range(1, 4):
        for hip_counter in range(1, 3):
            print('Hip')
        print('Hooray!')
```

The body of the outer loop is indented 4 spaces.

The loop variable of the inner loop is `hip_counter`.

The body of the inner loop is indented another 4 spaces.

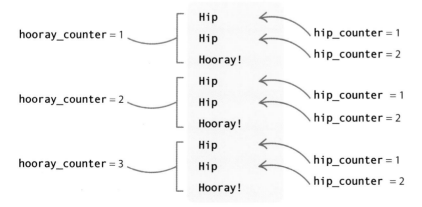

hooray_counter = 1

Hip — hip_counter = 1
Hip — hip_counter = 2
Hooray!

hooray_counter = 2

Hip — hip_counter = 1
Hip — hip_counter = 2
Hooray!

hooray_counter = 3

Hip — hip_counter = 1
Hip — hip_counter = 2
Hooray!

◁ **How it works**

The whole of the inner **for** loop is inside the body of the outer **for** loop. Each time we do one repeat of the outer loop, we have to do two repeats of the inner loop. This means the body of the outer loop is run three times in total, but the body of the inner loop is run six times.

Animal Quiz

Are you a fan of quizzes? Fancy making one yourself? In this project, you'll build an animal quiz. Even though the questions are about animals, this project can be easily modified to be about any other topic.

I thought I was the largest animal.

What happens

The program asks the player some questions about animals. They get three chances to answer each question – you don't want to make the quiz too difficult! Each correct answer will score one point. At the end of the quiz, the program reveals the player's final score.

This is how the game looks – it all happens in the shell window.

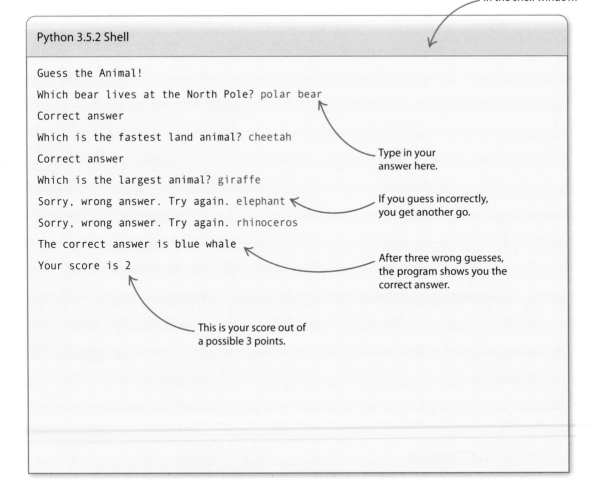

Python 3.5.2 Shell

```
Guess the Animal!
Which bear lives at the North Pole? polar bear
Correct answer
Which is the fastest land animal? cheetah
Correct answer
Which is the largest animal? giraffe
Sorry, wrong answer. Try again. elephant
Sorry, wrong answer. Try again. rhinoceros
The correct answer is blue whale
Your score is 2
```

Type in your answer here.

If you guess incorrectly, you get another go.

After three wrong guesses, the program shows you the correct answer.

This is your score out of a possible 3 points.

How it works

This project makes use of a function – a block of code with a name that performs a specific task. A function lets you use the same code repeatedly, without having to type it all in every time. Python has lots of built-in functions, but it also lets you create functions of your own.

▷ **Calling functions**

When you want to use a function, you "call it" by typing its name in your code. In Animal Quiz, you'll make a function that compares the player's guess to the true answer to see if it's correct. You'll call it for each question in the quiz.

▽ Animal Quiz flowchart

The program keeps checking whether there are any questions left to ask and whether the player has used up all of their chances. The score is stored in a variable during the game. Once all the questions have been answered, the game ends.

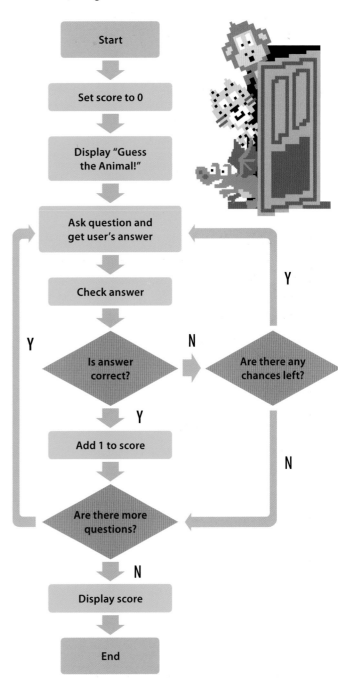

```
        Start
          ↓
    Set score to 0
          ↓
  Display "Guess
   the Animal!"
          ↓
  Ask question and  ←──────────────────────┐
  get user's answer ←──────────┐           │
          ↓                    │           │
    Check answer               │           │
          ↓                    │           │
   Y                    N      │           │
  Is answer    ──▷   Are there any         │
  correct?           chances left?         │
          ↓ Y                         N    │
    Add 1 to score              Y          │
          ↓                              │ │
  Are there more  ←──────────────────────┘ │
  questions?                                │
          ↓ N
   Display score
          ↓
        End
```

LINGO

Ignore the case!

When comparing the player's guess to the correct answer, it shouldn't matter if the player types capital letters or lower-case letters – all that matters is that the words are the same. This isn't true for all programs. For example, if a program that checks passwords ignores case, the passwords might become easier to guess, and less secure. However, in Animal Quiz, it doesn't matter if the player answers "bear" or "Bear" – both will be recognized as correct.

Putting it together

It's now time to build your quiz! First you'll create the questions and the mechanism for checking the answers. Then you'll add the code that gives the player three attempts to answer each question.

I hope I'm not venomous – I've just bitten my tongue!

1 **Create a new file**
Open IDLE. Under the File menu, select New File. Save the file as "animal_quiz.py".

> File
> Save
> Save As

2 **Create the score variable**
Type in the code shown here to create a variable called **score** and set its starting value to 0.

```
score = 0
```

You'll use this variable to keep track of the player's score.

3 **Introduce the game**
Next create a message to introduce the game to the player. This will be the first thing that the player sees on the screen.

This phrase will appear in the shell window.

```
score = 0
print('Guess the Animal!')
```

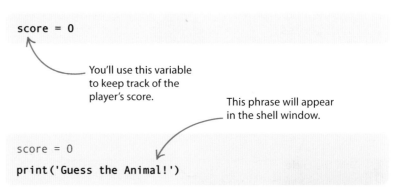

4 **Run the code**
Now try running the code. From the Run menu, choose Run Module. What happens next? You should see the welcome message in the shell window.

> Run
> Python Shell
> Check Module
> Run Module

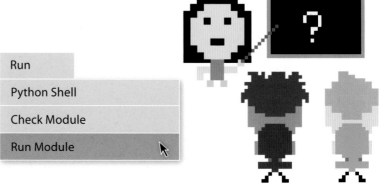

5 **Ask a question (user input)**
The next line of code asks a question and waits for the player's response. The answer (the user input) is saved in the variable **guess1**. Run the code to make sure the question appears.

```
print('Guess the Animal!')
guess1 = input('Which bear lives at the North Pole? ')
```

The variable **guess1** stores whatever the user types in.

6 **Build a check function**

The next task is to check if the player's guess is correct. Type this code at the top of your script, before **score = 0**. The code creates a function, called **check_guess()**, that will check if the player's guess matches the correct answer. The two words in brackets are "parameters" – bits of information the function needs. When you call a function, you assign (give) values to its parameters.

```
def check_guess(guess, answer):
    global score
    if guess == answer:
        print('Correct answer')
        score = score + 1
score = 0
```

The first line gives the function a name and parameters.

This line says the **score** variable is a global variable. It ensures that changes to the variable can be seen throughout the whole program.

Add 1 to the player's score.

Don't forget the brackets.

7 **Call the function**

Now add a line at the end of the script to "call" (run) the **check_guess()** function. This code tells the function to use the player's guess as the first parameter and the phrase "polar bear" as the second parameter.

```
guess1 = input('Which bear lives at the North Pole? ')
check_guess(guess1, 'polar bear')
```

Correct answer

8 **Test the code**

Try running the code again and type in the correct answer. The shell window should look like this.

```
Guess the Animal!
Which bear lives at the North Pole? polar bear
Correct answer
```

9 **Add some more questions**

It takes more than one question to make a quiz! Add two more questions to the program, following the same steps as before. We'll store the player's answers in the variables **guess2** and **guess3**.

Let me add some more.

```
score = 0
print('Guess the Animal!')
guess1 = input('Which bear lives at the North Pole? ')
check_guess(guess1, 'polar bear')
guess2 = input('Which is the fastest land animal? ')
check_guess(guess2, 'cheetah')
guess3 = input('Which is the largest animal? ')
check_guess(guess3, 'blue whale')
```

First question

This tells the program to check **guess1**.

This tells the program to check **guess3**.

10 **Display the score**

The next line of code will reveal the player's score in a message when the quiz ends. Add it to the bottom of the file, under the last question.

```python
guess3 = input('Which is the largest animal? ')
check_guess(guess3, 'blue whale')

print('Your score is ' + str(score))
```

This creates a message giving the player's score and displays it on the screen.

△ **How it works**

For this step, you have to use the **str()** function to change a number into a string. This is because Python shows an error if you try to add a string and an integer (whole number) together.

11 **Ignore case**

What happens if the player types "Lion" instead of "lion"? Will they still get a point? No, the code will tell them it's the wrong answer! To fix this, you need to make your code smarter. Python has a **lower()** function, which changes words into all lower-case characters. In your code, replace **if guess == answer:** with the line shown on the right in bold.

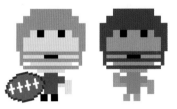

```python
def check_guess(guess, answer):
    global score
    if guess.lower() == answer.lower():
        print('Correct answer')
        score = score + 1
```

Change this line.

△ **How it works**

Both the guess and the answer will be converted into lower-case characters before being checked. This ensures that the code works whether the player uses all capital letters, all lower-case letters, or a mixture of the two.

12 **Test the code again**

Run your code for a third time. Try typing the correct answers using a mixture of capitals and lower-case letters and see what happens.

```
Guess the animal!
Which bear lives at the North Pole? polar bear
Correct answer
Which is the fastest land animal? Cheetah
Correct answer
Which is the largest animal? BLUE WHALE
Correct answer
Your score is 3
```

The case is ignored when deciding whether an answer is correct or not.

13 **Give the player more chances**

The player currently has only one chance to get the answer right. You can make it a bit easier for them by giving them three chances to answer a question. Change the `check_guess()` function to look like this.

Don't forget to save your work.

This variable will hold one of only two values: True or False.

```
def check_guess(guess, answer):
    global score
    still_guessing = True
    attempt = 0
    while still_guessing and attempt < 3:
        if guess.lower() == answer.lower():
            print('Correct answer')
            score = score + 1
            still_guessing = False
        else:
            if attempt < 2:
                guess = input('Sorry wrong answer. Try again. ')
            attempt = attempt + 1
    if attempt == 3:
        print('The correct answer is ' + answer)
score = 0
```

A `while` loop runs the check code three times or until the player gets the answer correct – whichever comes first.

Make sure each line of code has the correct indent.

The `else` variable asks the player to enter another answer if they get it wrong.

Add 1 to the number of guesses the player has had.

This code displays the correct answer after three wrong guesses.

△ **How it works**

To know if the player has got the right answer, you need to create a variable called **still_guessing**. You then set the variable to True to show that the right answer hasn't been found. It's set to False when the player gets the right answer.

Largest animal? I don't know. Give me three guesses!

Hacks and tweaks

Mix up your quiz! Make it longer or harder, use different types of questions, or even change the subject of the quiz. You can try any or all of these hacks and tweaks, but remember to save each one as a separate Python file so that you don't mess up the original game.

◁ **Make it longer**

Add more questions to the quiz. Some examples could be "Which animal has a long trunk?" (elephant) or "What kind of mammal can fly?" (bat). Or, a bit harder: "How many hearts does an octopus have?" (three).

Use a backslash character if you need to split a long line of code over two lines.

```
guess = input('Which one of these is a fish? \
A) Whale B) Dolphin C) Shark D) Squid. Type A, B, C, or D ')
check_guess(guess, 'C')
```

◁ **Make a multiple-choice quiz**

This code shows how to create multiple-choice questions, which give the player several possible answers to choose from.

REMEMBER

Breaking the line

You can use \n to make a new line anywhere. Multiple-choice questions are easier to understand if the question and possible answers appear on different lines. To show the fish question as a list of options, type it like this.

```
guess = input('Which one of these is a fish?\n \
A) Whale\n B) Dolphin\n C) Shark\n D) Squid\n \
Type A, B, C, or D ')
check_guess(guess, 'C')
```

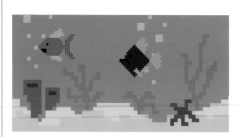

```
Which one of these is a fish?
  A) Whale
  B) Dolphin
  C) Shark
  D) Squid
Type A, B, C, or D
```

This is how the question appears in the shell window.

```
while still_guessing and attempt < 3:
    if guess.lower() == answer.lower():
        print('Correct Answer')
        score = score + 3 - attempt
        still_guessing = False
    else:
        if attempt < 2:
```

This line replaces `score + 1`.

◁ **Better score for fewer attempts**
Reward the player for getting the answer right with fewer guesses. Give 3 points if they get it in one go, 2 points for needing two attempts, and 1 point for using all three chances. Make this change to the line that updates the score. Now it will give 3 points minus the number of unsuccessful attempts. If the player gets the answer right first time, 3 – 0 = 3 points are added to their score; on the second guess, it's 3 – 1 = 2 points; and on the third guess, it's 3 – 2 = 1 point.

▷ **Make a true-or-false quiz**
This code shows how to create true-or-false questions, which have only two possible answers.

```
guess = input('Mice are mammals. True or False? ')
check_guess(guess, 'True')
```

▷ **Change the difficulty**
To make the quiz harder, give the player fewer chances to get the right answer. If you make a true-or-false quiz, you'll only want the player to have one guess per question, and perhaps no more than two guesses per question if it's a multiple-choice quiz. Can you figure out what you'd need to change the highlighted numbers to for true-or-false or multiple-choice questions?

```
def check_guess(guess, answer):
    global score
    still_guessing = True
    attempt = 0
    while still_guessing and attempt < 3:
        if guess.lower() == answer.lower():
            print('Correct Answer')
            score = score + 1
            still_guessing = False
        else:
            if attempt < 2:
                guess = input('Sorry wrong answer.Try again. ')
                attempt = attempt + 1
    if attempt == 3:
        print('The correct answer is ' + answer)
```

Change this number.

Change this number.

Change this number.

Not as easy as I thought it would be...

▷ **Choose another topic**
Create a quiz on a different subject, such as general knowledge, sports, movies, or music. You could even make a quiz about your family or friends and include some cheeky questions, like "Who has the most annoying laugh?"

Functions

Programmers love shortcuts that make writing code easier. One of the most common shortcuts is to give a name to a block of code that does an especially useful job. Then, instead of having to type out the whole block each time you need it, you simply type its name. These named blocks of code are called functions.

How to use a function

Using a function is also known as "calling" it. To call a function, you just type the function's name, followed by a set of brackets that contain any parameters you want the function to work with. Parameters are a bit like variables that belong to the function, and they allow you to pass data between different parts of your program. When a function doesn't need any parameters, the brackets are left empty.

LINGO

Function terms

There are a number of special words that coders use when talking about functions.

Call To use a function.

Define When you use the **def** keyword and write the code for a function, coders say you "define" the function. You also define a variable when you first set its value.

Parameter A piece of data (information) that you give to a function to use.

Return value Data that you pass from a function back to the main code. You get it using the keyword **return**.

Built-in functions

Python has a number of built-in functions that you can use in your code. These are helpful tools that let you do lots of tasks, from inputting information and showing messages on the screen to converting one type of data into another. You've already used some of Python's built-in functions, such as **print()** and **input()**. Have a look at these examples. Why not try them out in the shell?

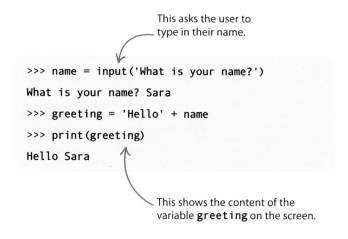

This asks the user to type in their name.

```
>>> name = input('What is your name?')
What is your name? Sara
>>> greeting = 'Hello' + name
>>> print(greeting)
Hello Sara
```

This shows the content of the variable **greeting** on the screen.

△ **input()** and **print()**

These two functions are like opposites. The **input()** function lets the user give instructions or data to the program by typing them in. The **print()** function sends output to the user by displaying messages or results on the screen.

▽ max()

The **max()** function selects the maximum value from the parameters you give it. Hit the enter/return key to see the value on the screen. This function takes multiple parameters, which must be separated by commas.

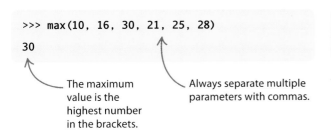

```
>>> max(10, 16, 30, 21, 25, 28)
30
```

The maximum value is the highest number in the brackets.

Always separate multiple parameters with commas.

▽ min()

The function **min()** does the opposite of **max()**. It selects the minimum value from the parameters you put inside its brackets. Experiment for yourself with the **max()** and **min()** functions.

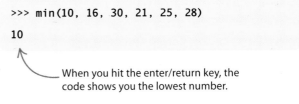

```
>>> min(10, 16, 30, 21, 25, 28)
10
```

When you hit the enter/return key, the code shows you the lowest number.

Another way of calling

Some of the different types of data we've come across so far, such as integers, strings, and lists, have their own functions. These functions must be called in a special way. You type the data or the name of the variable holding the data, followed by a dot, the function's name, and finally brackets. Test out these code snippets in the shell.

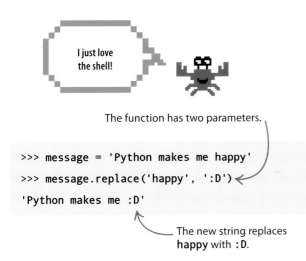

I just love the shell!

Don't forget the dot.

Empty brackets mean that no parameters are needed.

```
>>> 'bang'.upper()
'BANG'
```

This is the new string, all in capitals.

△ upper()

The **upper()** function takes an existing string and returns a new string in which all the lower-case characters are changed to upper-case (capitals).

The function has two parameters.

```
>>> message = 'Python makes me happy'
>>> message.replace('happy', ':D')
'Python makes me :D'
```

The new string replaces **happy** with **:D**.

△ replace()

Two parameters are needed for this function: the first is the part of a string you want to replace, while the second is the string you want to put in its place. The function returns a new string with the replacements made.

The list of numbers stored in the variable

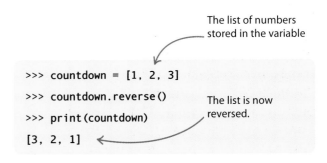

```
>>> countdown = [1, 2, 3]
>>> countdown.reverse()
>>> print(countdown)
[3, 2, 1]
```

The list is now reversed.

△ reverse()

Use this function when you want to reverse the order of the items in a list. Here, it's used to reverse a list of numbers stored in the variable **countdown**. Instead of printing the list as **[1, 2, 3]**, the function makes it print **[3, 2, 1]**.

Making a function

The best functions have a clear purpose and a good name that explains what they do – think of the **check_guess()** function you used in Animal Quiz. Follow these instructions to create, or "define", a function that calculates the number of seconds in a day and then prints the answer on the screen.

The keyword **def** tells Python that this block of code is a function.

The lines after the name must be indented 4 spaces, to show Python that they are part of the function.

This command calls the function.

1 Define the function

Create a new file in IDLE. Save it as "functions.py". Type these lines into the editor window. An indent is added at the start of each line in the function. Save the file again, then run the code to see what happens.

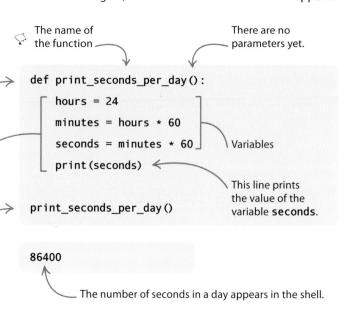

The name of the function

There are no parameters yet.

```
def print_seconds_per_day():
    hours = 24
    minutes = hours * 60
    seconds = minutes * 60
    print(seconds)

print_seconds_per_day()
```

Variables

This line prints the value of the variable **seconds**.

```
86400
```

The number of seconds in a day appears in the shell.

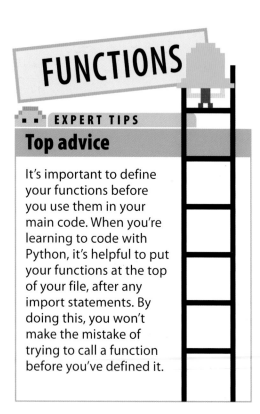

FUNCTIONS

■ ■ **EXPERT TIPS**

Top advice

It's important to define your functions before you use them in your main code. When you're learning to code with Python, it's helpful to put your functions at the top of your file, after any import statements. By doing this, you won't make the mistake of trying to call a function before you've defined it.

2 Add parameters

If you want to give your function any values to work with, you put them inside the brackets as parameters. For example, to find out the total number of seconds in a particular number of days, change your code to look like this. The function now has the parameter **days**. You can specify the number of days when you call the function. Try it out yourself.

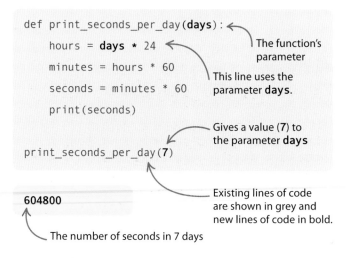

```
def print_seconds_per_day(days):
    hours = days * 24
    minutes = hours * 60
    seconds = minutes * 60
    print(seconds)

print_seconds_per_day(7)
```

The function's parameter

This line uses the parameter **days**.

Gives a value (**7**) to the parameter **days**

Existing lines of code are shown in grey and new lines of code in bold.

```
604800
```

The number of seconds in 7 days

3 **Return a value**

Once you have a function that does something useful, you'll want to use the results from that function in the rest of your code. You can get values out of a function by "returning" them. Change your code as shown here to get the return value from your function. You should rename the function to match its new purpose. Don't try to run the code just yet.

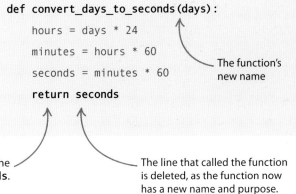

```
def convert_days_to_seconds(days):
    hours = days * 24
    minutes = hours * 60
    seconds = minutes * 60
    return seconds
```

The function's new name

The keyword **return** gives the value of the variable **seconds**.

The line that called the function is deleted, as the function now has a new name and purpose.

This calls the function and gives a value (**7**) to the parameter **days**.

4 **Store and use the return value**

You can store the return value from a function in a variable to use later in your code. Add this code under your function. It stores the return value and uses it to calculate the number of milliseconds (thousandths of a second). Try it out and experiment with the number of days.

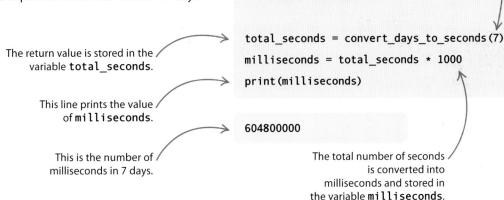

```
def convert_days_to_seconds(days):
    hours = days * 24
    minutes = hours * 60
    seconds = minutes * 60
    return seconds
```

The return value is stored in the variable **total_seconds**.

This line prints the value of **milliseconds**.

```
total_seconds = convert_days_to_seconds(7)
milliseconds = total_seconds * 1000
print(milliseconds)
```

```
604800000
```

This is the number of milliseconds in 7 days.

The total number of seconds is converted into milliseconds and stored in the variable **milliseconds**.

EXPERT TIPS

Naming your functions

In Step 3, you changed the name of your function from **print_seconds_per_day()** to **convert_days_to_seconds()**. Just like with variables, it's important that the name you use accurately explains what the function does. This makes your code much easier to understand.

The rules for naming functions are similar to those for variables. Function names can contain letters, numbers, and underscores, but they should begin with a letter. If there are several words in the name, the words should be separated by underscores.

Fixing bugs

If something's wrong with your code, Python will try to help by showing an error message. These messages can seem a bit puzzling at first, but they'll give you clues about why your program isn't working and how to fix it.

Error messages

Both the IDLE editor and the shell window can show error messages if mistakes are detected. An error message tells you what type of error has occurred and where to look in your code.

▽ **Messages in the shell**

Python displays error messages in red text in the shell window. The program stops working when an error message appears. The message tells you which line of code caused the error to happen.

▽ **Messages in the IDLE editor**

A pop-up box warns you there's an error. Click "OK" to return to your program. There will be a red highlight on or near the error.

This pop-up box tells you there's a syntax error, which means there's a typing mistake.

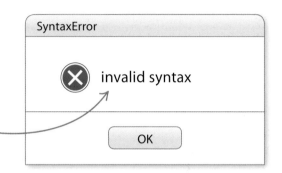

```
SyntaxError

    ⊗   invalid syntax

                    OK
```

```
>>>

Traceback (most recent call last):
    File "Users/Craig/Developments/top-secret-python-book/age.py", line 21, in module>
        print('I am'+ age + 'years old')
TypeError: Can't convert 'int' object to str implicitly
```

This line tells you it's a type error (see page 50).

The error is on line 21.

I'll find those pesky bugs!

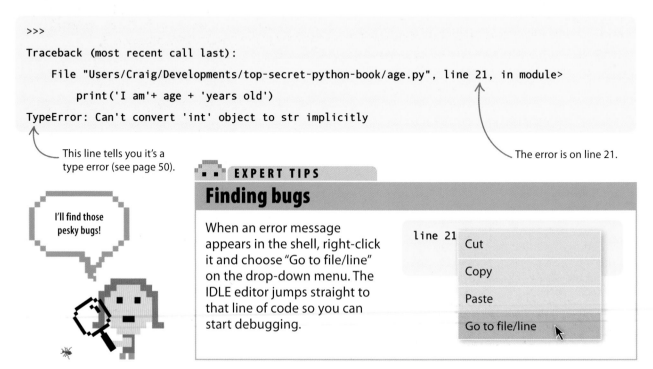

EXPERT TIPS

Finding bugs

When an error message appears in the shell, right-click it and choose "Go to file/line" on the drop-down menu. The IDLE editor jumps straight to that line of code so you can start debugging.

```
line 21
            Cut

            Copy

            Paste

            Go to file/line
```

Syntax errors

When you get a syntax error message, it's a hint that you've typed something incorrectly. Perhaps your fingers slipped and hit a wrong letter? Don't worry – these are the easiest errors to fix. Check through your code carefully and try to spot what went wrong.

The closing bracket is missing – it needs another curved bracket here.

```
input('What is your name?'
```

The first quotation mark is missing. It needs to be a single quote to match.

```
print(It is your turn')
```

▷ **Things to look out for**
Are you missing a bracket or quotation mark? Do your pairs of brackets and quotation marks match? Have you made a spelling mistake? All these things can cause syntax errors.

This is a spelling mistake – it should be **short_shots**.

```
total_score = (long_shots * 3) + (shoort_shots * 2)
```

Indentation errors

Python uses indentation to understand where blocks of code start and stop. An indentation error means something is wrong with the way you've structured the code. Remember: if a line of code ends with a colon (:), the next line must be indented. Press the space bar four times to manually indent a line.

```
if weekday is True:
print('Go to school')
```

This line of code would trigger an indentation error message.

Four spaces

```
if weekday is True:
    print('Go to school')
```

You need to indent the code on the second line like this to fix the error.

▽ **Indent each new block**
In your Python programs, you'll often have one block of code within another block, such as a loop that sits inside a function. Every line in a particular block must be indented by the same amount. Although Python helps by automatically indenting after colons, you still need to check that each block is indented correctly.

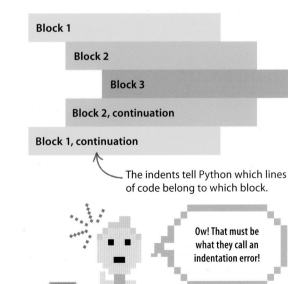

Block 1
Block 2
Block 3
Block 2, continuation
Block 1, continuation

The indents tell Python which lines of code belong to which block.

Ow! That must be what they call an indentation error!

Type errors

A type error isn't a typing error – it means your code has muddled up one type of data with another type, such as confusing numbers with strings. It's like trying to bake a cake in your fridge – it won't work, because the fridge isn't meant for baking! If you ask Python to do something impossible, don't be surprised if it won't cooperate!

I thought they were taking a long time to cook!

FRIDGE

```
budget = 'Fifty' * 'Five'
```

You can multiply two numbers in Python, but you can't do multiplication with strings.

◁ **Examples of type errors**
Type errors occur when you ask Python to do something that doesn't make sense to it, such as multiplying with strings, comparing two completely different types of data, or telling it to find a number in a list of letters.

```
hot_day = '20 degrees' > 15
```

Python can't check to see if a string is greater than a number, as they are different data types.

You can't do multiplication with strings!

```
list = ['a','b','c']
find_biggest_number(list)
```

This function is expecting you to give it a list of numbers, but you've given it a list of letters instead!

Name errors

A name error message appears if your code uses the name of a variable or function that hasn't yet been created. To avoid this, always define your variables and functions before you write code to use them. It's good practice to define all your functions at the top of your program.

▷ **Name errors**
A name error in this code stops Python from displaying the message "I live in Moscow". You need to create the variable **hometown** first, before you use the **print()** function.

The **print()** instruction needs to come after the variable.

```
print('I live in ' + hometown)
hometown = 'Moscow'
```

Logic errors

Sometimes you can tell something has gone wrong even if Python hasn't given you an error message, because your program isn't doing what you expected. It could be that you've got a logic error. You may have typed in the code correctly, but if you missed an important line or put the instructions in the wrong order it won't run properly.

Logic error! Does not compute...

```python
print('Oh no! You have lost a life')
print(lives)
lives = lives - 1
```

All the lines of code are correct, but two are in the wrong order.

◁ **Can you spot the bug?**
This code will run with no error messages, but there's a logic error in it. The value of `lives` is shown on the screen before the number of lives is reduced by one. The player of this game will see the wrong number of lives remaining! To fix it, move the instruction `print(lives)` to the end.

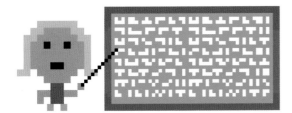

◁ **Line by line**
Logic errors can be tricky to find, but as you get more experienced you'll get good at tracking them down. Try to identify logic errors by checking your code slowly, line by line. Be patient and take your time – you'll find the problem in the end.

Bug-busting checklist

Sometimes you might think that you'll never get a program to work, but don't give up! If you follow the tips in this handy checklist, you'll be able to identify most errors.

Ask yourself...
- If you build one of the projects in this book and it doesn't work, check that the code you've typed matches the book exactly.
- Is everything spelled correctly?
- Do you have unnecessary spaces at the start of a line?
- Have you confused any numbers for letters, such as 0 and O?
- Have you used upper-case and lower-case letters in the right places?
- Do all open brackets have a matching closing bracket? ( ) [ ] { }
- Do all single and double quotes have a matching closing quote? ' ' " "
- Have you asked someone else to check your code against the book?
- Have you saved your code since you last made changes?

Password Picker

Passwords stop other people from accessing our computers, personal emails, and website login details. In this project, you'll build a tool that makes secure, memorable passwords to help keep your private information safe.

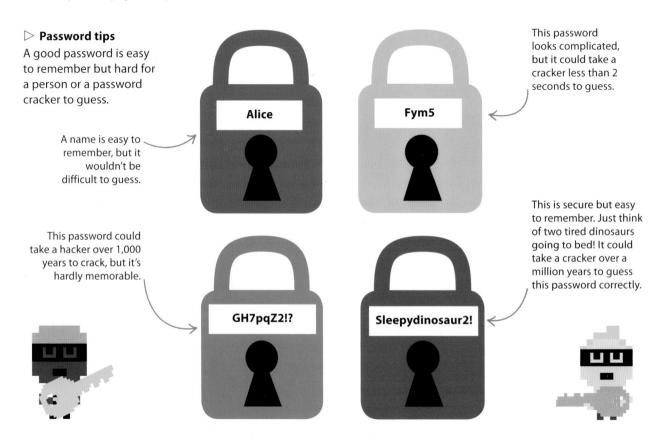

▷ **Password tips**
A good password is easy to remember but hard for a person or a password cracker to guess.

A name is easy to remember, but it wouldn't be difficult to guess.

Alice

Fym5

This password looks complicated, but it could take a cracker less than 2 seconds to guess.

This password could take a hacker over 1,000 years to crack, but it's hardly memorable.

GH7pqZ2!?

Sleepydinosaur2!

This is secure but easy to remember. Just think of two tired dinosaurs going to bed! It could take a cracker over a million years to guess this password correctly.

What happens

Password Picker will enable you to create strong passwords by combining words, numbers, and characters. When you run the program, it will create a new password and show it on the screen. You can ask it to keep creating new passwords until you find one you like.

LINGO
Password cracker

A cracker is a program used by hackers to guess passwords. Some crackers can make millions of guesses every second. A cracker usually starts by guessing commonly used words and names. An unusual password made up of several different parts will help protect against crackers.

▽ Password Picker flowchart

The program randomly selects each of the password's four parts, puts them together, and displays the password in the shell window. If you want another password, it repeats those steps again. If you don't, the program ends.

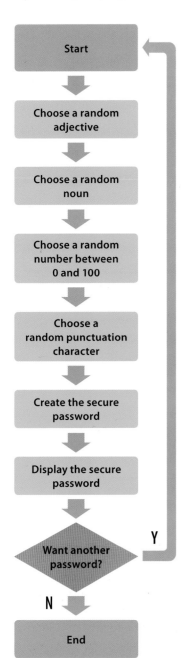

How it works

This project will show you how to use Python's **random** module. The program uses random choices from groups of adjectives, nouns, numbers, and punctuation characters to assemble each password. You'll soon be making crazy, hard-to-forget passwords, such as "fluffyapple14(" or "smellygoat&"!

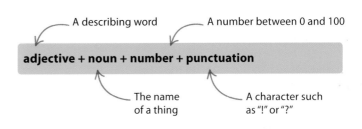

A describing word

A number between 0 and 100

adjective + noun + number + punctuation

The name of a thing

A character such as "!" or "?"

Clever yet simple!

The program does clever things with passwords, but there isn't a lot of code in it, so it won't take long to make.

That string is totally Random!

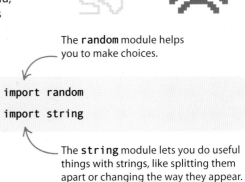

1 Create a new file
Open IDLE. Under the File menu, select New File. Save the file as "password_picker.py".

The **random** module helps you to make choices.

```
import random
import string
```

The **string** module lets you do useful things with strings, like splitting them apart or changing the way they appear.

2 Add the modules
Import the **string** and **random** modules from the Python library. Type these two lines at the top of your file, so you can use the modules later.

This line shows a message to welcome the user.

3 Welcome the user
First create a message to welcome the user to the program.

```
import random
import string
print('Welcome to Password Picker!')
```

4 **Try out the code**
Run your code. The welcome message should appear in the shell window.

```
Welcome to Password Picker!
```

5 **Make an adjective list**
You'll need adjectives and nouns to generate new passwords. In Python, you can keep a group of related things together as a list. First create the variable **adjectives** to store your list by typing this new block of code between the **print()** command and the **import** statements. Put the whole list in square brackets, and separate each item with a comma.

The list is stored in the variable **adjectives**.

Each item is a string.

Put a comma after each item.

```
import string

adjectives = ['sleepy', 'slow', 'smelly',
              'wet', 'fat', 'red',
              'orange', 'yellow', 'green',
              'blue', 'purple', 'fluffy',
              'white', 'proud', 'brave']

print('Welcome to Password Picker!')
```

The list is in square brackets.

6 **Make a noun list**
Next create a variable that holds a list of nouns. Put it under the adjective list and above the **print()** command. Remember to use commas and square brackets, like you did in Step 5.

```
                      'white', 'proud', 'brave']

nouns = ['apple', 'dinosaur', 'ball',
         'toaster', 'goat', 'dragon',
         'hammer', 'duck', 'panda']

print('Welcome to Password Picker!')
```

Use commas and square brackets.

EXPERT TIPS
Random numbers

Rolling a dice, picking a card from a deck, or tossing a coin are all things you can simulate by generating a random number. You can read more about how to use Python's random module in the "Docs" section of the "Help" menu.

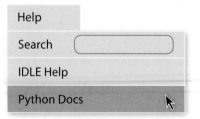

| Help |
| Search |
| IDLE Help |
| Python Docs |

7 **Pick the words**
To create the password, you'll need to pick a random adjective and a random noun. You do this using the **choice()** function from the random module. Type this code below the **print()** command. (You can use this function any time you want to select a random item from a list. Just give it the variable containing the items.)

```
print('Welcome to Password Picker!')

adjective = random.choice(adjectives)
noun = random.choice(nouns)
```

This variable holds a word chosen randomly from the adjectives list.

One of the nouns from the list is chosen and stored in this variable.

8 **Select a number**
Now use the **randrange()** function from the random module to select a random number from 0 to 100. Put this line at the bottom of your code.

```
noun = random.choice(nouns)
number = random.randrange(0, 100)
```

9 **Select a special character**
Using the **random.choice()** function again, add this line to pick a random punctuation character. This will make your password even harder to crack!

```
number = random.randrange(0, 100)
special_char = random.choice(string.punctuation)
```

This is a constant.

EXPERT TIPS
Constants

A constant is a special type of variable whose contents can't be changed. The constant **string.punctuation** holds a string of characters used for punctuation. To see what it holds, type **import string** into the shell, followed by **print(string.punctuation)**.

```
>>> import string
>>> print(string.punctuation)
!"#$%&'()*+,-./:;<=>?@[\]^_`{|}~
```

Characters in this constant

Your secure password will be stored in this variable.

This changes the random number into a string.

10 **Create the new secure password**
It's time to assemble all the different parts to create the new secure password. Type these two lines of code at the end of your program.

```
password = adjective + noun + str(number) + special_char
print('Your new password is: %s' % password)
```

This displays the new password in the shell.

EXPERT TIPS
Strings and integers

The **str()** function turns a whole number (an integer) into a string. If you don't use this function, Python shows an error when you try to add an integer to a string. Test it: type **print('route '+66)** into the shell window.

```
>>> print('route '+66)
Traceback (most recent call last):
    File '<pyshell#0>', line 1, in <module>
        print('route '+66)
TypeError: Can't convert 'int' object to str implicitly
```

Error message

To avoid this error, use the **str()** function to change the number into a string first.

```
>>> print('route '+str(66))
route 66
```

The number goes inside the brackets of the **str()** function.

11 Test the program
This is a good point to test your code. Run it and look in the shell to see the result. If you have errors, don't worry. Look back over your code carefully to spot any mistakes.

```
Welcome to Password Picker!

Your new password is: bluegoat92=
```

Your random password will probably be different.

Don't forget to save your work.

12 Another one?
You can use a `while` loop to generate another password if the user says they want a different one. Add this code to your program. It asks the user if they require a new password, then stores the reply in a variable called **response**.

```python
print('Welcome to Password Picker!')

while True:
    adjective = random.choice(adjectives)
    noun = random.choice(nouns)
    number = random.randrange(0, 100)
    special_char = random.choice(string.punctuation)

    password = adjective + noun + str(number) + special_char
    print('Your new password is: %s' % password)

    response = input('Would you like another password? Type y or n: ')
    if response == 'n':
        break
```

The `while` loop starts here.

You need to indent these existing lines to make sure they're in the `while` loop.

The `while` loop ends here.

The `input ()` function asks the user to enter a response into the shell.

If the answer's "yes" (**y**), the loop returns to the start. If it's "no" (**n**), the program exits the loop.

13 Pick a perfect password
That's it – you've finished. Now you can create hard-to-crack passwords that are fun to remember!

```
Welcome to Password Picker!
Your new password is: yellowapple42}
Would you like another password? Type y or n: y
Your new password is: greenpanda13*
Would you like another password? Type y or n: n
```

Type "**y**" at this prompt to get a new password.

Type "**n**" at this prompt to quit the program.

Hacks and tweaks

Have a go at remixing your program to add these extra features. Can you think of any other ways to make it even more cracker-proof?

I'll never find the right key!

▷ **Add more words**

To increase the number of possible passwords, add more words to the lists of nouns and adjectives. Think of unusual or silly words that will stick in your mind if they appear in a password.

```
nouns = ['apple', 'dinosaur', 'ball',
         'toaster', 'goat', 'dragon',
         'hammer', 'duck', 'panda',
         'telephone', 'banana', 'teacher']
```

```
while True:

    for num in range(3):
        adjective = random.choice(adjectives)
        noun = random.choice(nouns)
        number = random.randrange(0, 100)
        special_char = random.choice(string.punctuation)

        password = adjective + noun + str(number) + special_char
        print('Your new password is: %s' % password)

    response = input('Would you like more passwords? Type y or n: ')
```

The **for** loop runs 3 times, and selects 3 different passwords.

Keep these lines indented.

△ **Get multiple passwords**

Change the code so your program will create and display three passwords at once. You will need to use a **for** loop. Put it inside the **while** loop.

Mmm! Hairy, blue potatoes!

▷ **Make it longer**

Make the password longer and more secure by adding another word into each password. You could create a list of colours, then select a random colour to add to each password.

Add a random colour.

```
Your new password is: hairybluepotato33%
```

Modules

Modules are bundles of ready-made code that help you deal with common coding challenges. Modules provide the less exciting bits of code, letting you focus on the fun stuff. Also, because modules are used by a lot of people, they are likely to work well and be free of bugs.

Built-in modules

There are lots of useful modules included with Python. This collection of modules is known as the Standard Library. Here are some interesting modules from the library that you might want to experiment with.

△ **statistics**

Use **statistics** to calculate averages or find the most common value in a list of numbers. It's handy if you need to work out an average score in a game.

▷ **random**

You used this module to make random selections in Password Picker. It's great for adding an element of chance to a game or program.

▷ **socket**

The **socket** module allows programs to communicate across networks and the Internet. It could be used to create an online game.

▷ **datetime**

This module lets you work with dates. You can get today's date, or work out how long it is until a special day.

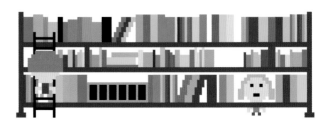

▷ **webbrowser**

You can control the computer's web browser with this module, allowing you to open web pages directly from your code.

This is the best one so far!

Using a module

To use a module in your code, you have to tell Python that you would like to include it. You instruct Python which modules to include using import statements. There are a few different ways that you can do this, depending on what you need from the module.

This line imports the whole **webbrowser** module.

▷ **import...**
Typing the keyword **import** allows you to use all the contents of a module. However, you need to put the module's name before any function you use. This code imports all the **webbrowser** module and uses its **open()** function to open the Python website in the computer's browser.

```
>>> import webbrowser
>>> webbrowser.open('https://docs.python.org/3/library')
```

The name of the module comes before the function.

Only the **choice** function is imported from the **random** module.

▷ **from... import...**
If you only want to use a particular part of a module, you can import just that part by adding the **from** keyword. Now you can just use the function name on its own. This code imports the **random** module's **choice()** function. The function picks a random item from any list you give it.

```
>>> from random import choice
>>> direction = choice(['N', 'S', 'E', 'W'])
>>> print(direction)
W
```

No module name is needed.

The code prints a random direction.

This line imports and renames the **time()** function.

▷ **from... import... a...**
Sometimes you may want to change the name of an imported module or function, perhaps because you've already used that name or maybe it isn't clear enough. To do this, use the **as** keyword followed by the new name. In the example shown here, the **time()** function, which we've renamed **time_now()**, gives us the current time. The time given is the exact number of seconds since 00:00 on 1 January 1970 – a date used by most computers as the start of their clock.

```
>>> from time import time as time_now
>>> now = time_now()
>>> print(now)
1478092571.003539
```

This variable uses the function's new name.

The number of seconds since 00:00 on 1 January 1970

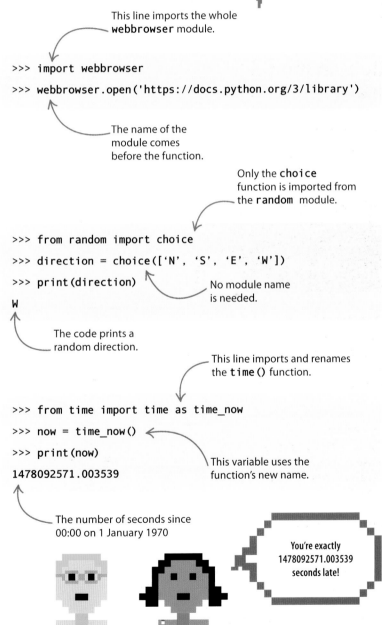

You're exactly 1478092571.003539 seconds late!

Nine Lives

In this nerve-shredding game, you have to guess the secret word one letter at a time. If your guess is wrong, you lose a life. Choose your letters carefully, as you only have nine lives. Lose all your lives, and it's game over!

What happens

The program shows you a mystery word with its letters replaced by question marks. If you guess a letter correctly, the program replaces the question mark with the correct letter. When you think you know what the word is, type it out in full. The game ends once you enter the correct word or have no lives left.

The clue shows the mystery word as question marks.

The number of lives you have left is shown by hearts.

```
['?', '?', '?', '?', '?']
Lives left: ♥♥♥♥♥♥♥♥♥
Guess a letter or the whole word: a
['?', '?', '?', '?', 'a']
Lives left: ♥♥♥♥♥♥♥♥♥
Guess a letter or the whole word: i
['?', 'i', '?', '?', 'a']
Lives left: ♥♥♥♥♥♥♥♥♥
Guess a letter or the whole word: y
Incorrect. You lose a life
['?', 'i', '?', '?', 'a']
Lives left: ♥♥♥♥♥♥♥♥
Guess a letter or the whole word: p
['p', 'i', '?', '?', 'a']
Lives left: ♥♥♥♥♥♥♥♥
Guess a letter or the whole word: t
Incorrect. You lose a life
['p', 'i', '?', '?', 'a']
Lives left: ♥♥♥♥♥♥♥
Guess a letter or the whole word: pizza
You won! The secret word was pizza
```

Each correct letter guessed reveals one or more letters in the secret word.

Each wrong guess makes a heart disappear.

If you know the word, type it in to win the game.

You have seven lives remaining. What's your next guess?

I guess "P"!

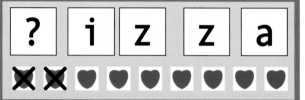

How it works

First you'll create two lists: one to store the secret words and one to store the clue, which is made up of question marks. Then, using the **random** module, you'll make a random selection from the list of secret words. Next you'll build a loop to check the player's guesses, and also create a function to update the clue as the word is slowly revealed.

◁ **Nine Lives flowchart**
The flowchart looks complicated, but the code for this game is relatively short. The main body of the program is a loop that checks the guessed letters to see if they are part of the secret word, and if the player has any lives left.

I've already got nine lives!

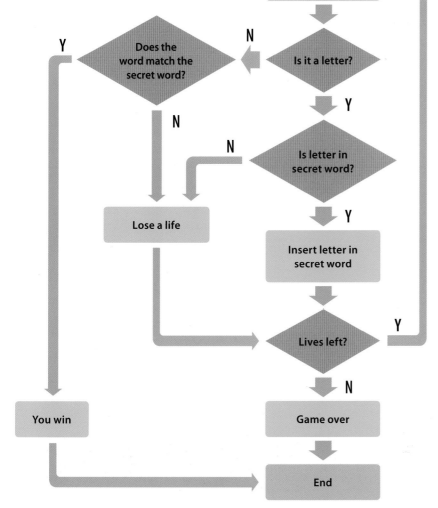

```
Start
  ↓
Set lives to 9
  ↓
Randomly select secret word
  ↓
Guess a letter or word  ←─────────────┐
  ↓                                    │
Is it a letter? ──N──→ Does the word match the secret word?
  │Y                      │Y            │N
  ↓                       │          Lose a life
Is letter in secret word? ──N──┐       │
  │Y                            │       │
  ↓                            Lose a life
Insert letter in secret word   │       │
  ↓                            │       │
Lives left? ←──────────────────┘───────┘
  │N          │Y──────────────────────┘
  ↓
Game over
  ↓
End  ←── You win
```

- Does the word match the secret word? — Y → You win
- Does the word match the secret word? — N → Lose a life
- Is it a letter? — N → Does the word match the secret word?
- Is it a letter? — Y → Is letter in secret word?
- Is letter in secret word? — N → Lose a life
- Is letter in secret word? — Y → Insert letter in secret word
- Lives left? — Y → Guess a letter or word
- Lives left? — N → Game over

Unicode characters

The letters, numbers, punctuation, and symbols that can be displayed on a computer are known as characters. There are characters for most of the world's languages and special characters for simple pictures, including emoji. Characters come in sets. For example, the ASCII (American Standard Code for Information Interchange) character set is used for the English language. For the hearts in this project you'll use the Unicode character set, which contains lots of different symbols, including the ones below.

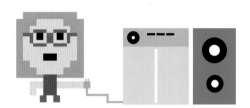

Setting up

You'll build Nine Lives in two stages. First you'll import the module you need for the program and create several variables. Then you'll write the main code for the program.

1 Create a new file
Open IDLE and create a new file. Save it as "nine_lives.py".

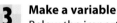

| File |
| Save |
| Save As |

2 Import the module
This project uses Python's **random** module, so start by typing the line of code shown here to import it.

```
import random
```

3 Make a variable
Below the import line, create a variable called **lives** to keep track of the number of lives (guesses) the player has left.

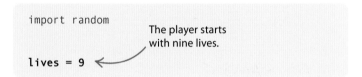

```
import random


lives = 9
```
The player starts with nine lives.

4 Make a list
The program will only know the words that you give to it. You'll need to put these words in a list, then store the list in a variable called **words**. Add this line beneath your **lives** variable.

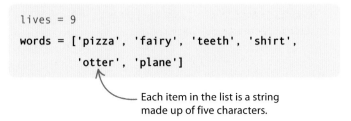

```
lives = 9
words = ['pizza', 'fairy', 'teeth', 'shirt',
         'otter', 'plane']
```
Each item in the list is a string made up of five characters.

5 Choose a secret word
At the start of each game, the program will randomly pick the word that the player has to guess and store it in a variable called **secret_word**. Add a line to create this new variable.

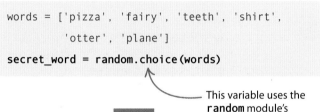

```
words = ['pizza', 'fairy', 'teeth', 'shirt',
         'otter', 'plane']
secret_word = random.choice(words)
```
This variable uses the **random** module's **choice** function.

Pick any card at random.

Store the clue

Now create another list to hold the clue. Unknown letters are stored as question marks. These will be replaced when the player guesses a letter correctly. At the start of the game, the whole list is question marks. You could write it as `clue = list['?', '?', '?', '?', '?']`, typing one question mark for each letter in the secret word, but the code below is a faster way to write it. Add this line after the `secret_word` variable.

```
secret_word = random.choice(words)
clue = list('?????')
```

The five question marks are stored as a list in the variable `clue`.

> I've stored all the clues.

 Show the lives left

This project uses the Unicode heart character to display how many lives are left. To make your program easier to read and write, add the next line of code to store the character in a variable.

```
clue = list('?????')
heart_symbol = u'\u2764'
```

Remember the result

Now make a variable to store whether or not the player has guessed the word correctly. The variable is set as `False` to begin with because the player doesn't know the word when the game starts. Type this line below the code for the heart symbol.

```
heart_symbol = u'\u2764'
guessed_word_correctly = False
```

This is a Boolean (True or False) value.

> • • ■ **EXPERT TIPS**
> # Word length

Be careful to only add words that are five letters long. The list that stores the clue only has room for five characters. If you add words of more than five letters, you'll see an error message when the program tries to enter any letters past the fifth one in the clue.

```
Index error: list assignment index
out of range
```

If you try to add words that are less than five letters long, the program will work, but the player will still see five question marks. They'll think that the answer has to be five letters long. For example, if you used "car", the program would look like this.

```
['?', '?', '?', '?', '?']
Lives left: ♥♥♥♥♥♥♥♥♥
Guess a letter or the whole word: c
['c', '?', '?', '?', '?']
Lives left: ♥♥♥♥♥♥♥♥♥
Guess a letter or the whole word: a
['c', 'a', '?', '?', '?']
Lives left: ♥♥♥♥♥♥♥♥♥
Guess a letter or the whole word: r
['c', 'a', 'r', '?', '?']
Lives left: ♥♥♥♥♥♥♥♥♥
Guess a letter or the whole word: |
```

The last two question marks don't represent any letters, so they never disappear.

The player could never win, because the last two question marks would remain no matter what letter they guessed!

The main code

The main part of the code is a loop that gets a letter from the player and checks if it's in the secret word. If it is, the code uses a function to update the clue. You'll make that function, then create the main loop.

9 **Is the letter in the secret word?**
If the guessed letter is in the secret word, you must update the clue. To do this, you'll use a function called `update_clue()`. The function has three parameters: the letter being guessed, the secret word, and the clue. Add this code after the `guessed_word_correctly` variable.

▷ **How it works**

The function contains a `while` loop that works through the secret word one letter at a time, checking whether each letter matches the guessed letter. The index variable keeps count of the current letter as the program scans through the word.

If a letter matches, the program inserts it into the clue, using `index` to find the right position in the list of question marks.

```
guessed_word_correctly = False


def update_clue(guessed_letter, secret_word, clue):
    index = 0
    while index < len(secret_word):
        if guessed_letter == secret_word[index]:
            clue[index] = guessed_letter
        index = index + 1
```

`len()` returns how many letters are in a word – in this case five.

Add 1 to the index value.

10 **Guess a letter or word**
Your program should keep asking the user to guess a letter or the whole word until they either get the correct answer or run out of lives. This is what the main loop does. Add this code below the `update_clue()` function.

This shows the clue and how many lives the player has left.

If the guessed letter is in the secret word, the clue is updated.

If the guess is incorrect (`else`), the number of lives is reduced by 1.

```
    index = index + 1


while lives > 0:
    print(clue)
    print('Lives left: ' + heart_symbol * lives)
    guess = input('Guess a letter or the whole word: ')

    if guess == secret_word:
        guessed_word_correctly = True
        break

    if guess in secret_word:
        update_clue(guess, secret_word, clue)
    else:
        print('Incorrect. You lose a life')
        lives = lives - 1
```

The loop keeps running while there are lives left.

This gets the guessed letter or word from the player.

When the word is guessed correctly, this line breaks the loop.

Repeating a string

The code `print('Lives left: ' + heart_symbol * lives)` uses a neat trick to display a heart for each remaining life. You can tell Python to repeat a string a specific number of times by multiplying it by a number. For example, `print(heart_symbol * 10)` would display ten hearts. Try this code out in the shell.

```
>>> heart_symbol = u'\u2764'
>>> print(heart_symbol * 10)
♥♥♥♥♥♥♥♥♥♥
```

11 Did you win?

When the game ends, you need to work out if the player has won. If the `guessed_word_correctly` variable is `True`, you know the loop ended before the player ran out of lives – so they've won the game. Otherwise `(else)`, they've lost. Add this code to the end of your program.

Yay, I won!

```
        lives = lives - 1

if guessed_word_correctly:

    print('You won! The secret word was ' + secret_word)
else:
    print('You lost! The secret word was ' + secret_word)
```

This is shorthand for "`if guessed_word_correctly = True`"

Don't forget to save your work.

12 Test your code

Try the game to make sure it runs OK. If there's a problem, carefully check your code for bugs. When you've got it working, invite your friends to take the Nine Lives challenge!

```
['?', '?', '?', '?', '?']
Lives left: ♥♥♥♥♥♥♥♥♥
Guess a letter or the whole word:
```

Just type a letter to start playing!

I'd like to take it for a test drive.

Hacks and tweaks

There are lots of ways you can remix and adapt this game. You can add new words, change the word length, or make it easier or harder.

▽ **Add more words**

Try adding more words to the program's word list. You can add as many as you want, but remember to only use words that are five letters long.

```
words = ['pizza', 'fairy', 'teeth', 'shirt', 'otter', 'plane', 'brush', 'horse', 'light']
```

▽ **Change the number of lives**

You can make it easier or harder for the player by giving them more or fewer lives. To do this, simply change the lives variable that you created in Step 3.

More lives?
Yes please!

Mississippi

◁ **Use longer words**

If you think using only five-letter words makes the game too easy, switch to words that are a bit longer – but remember to keep them all the same length. To make the game fiendishly difficult, search a dictionary for the longest and most unusual words you can find!

Add difficulty levels

To make the game more interesting, let the player choose the difficulty level at the start of the game. The easier setting gives the player more lives.

I wish I'd chosen
an easier route!

1 **Get the level**

Put this code at the start of your main program, just above the **while** loop. It asks the player to choose a level.

```
difficulty = input('Choose difficulty (type 1, 2 or 3):\n 1 Easy\n 2 Normal\n 3 Hard\n')
difficulty = int(difficulty)
```
difficulty is currently a string.
This line changes it to an integer.

```
while lives > 0:
```

2 Test the code

Run the program to check if this change works. You should see this message appear in the shell window.

```
Choose difficulty (type 1, 2, or 3):
 1 Easy
 2 Normal
 3 Hard
```

3 Set the levels

Now use `if`, `elif`, and `else` statements to set the number of lives for each level. Try using 12 lives for easy, 9 for normal, and 6 for hard. If you're not happy with how easy or hard the levels are, you can change the number of lives after you've tested them out. Add this code after the lines that ask the player to choose a level.

I'll try a harder workout today!

```python
difficulty = input('Choose difficulty (type 1, 2 or 3):\n 1 Easy\n 2 Normal\n 3 Hard\n')
difficulty = int(difficulty)

if difficulty == 1:
    lives = 12
elif difficulty == 2:
    lives = 9
else:
    lives = 6
```

Words of varying length

What if you want to play a game with varying word lengths? If you don't know the length of the secret word before the program is run, you won't know how long to make the list to hold the clue. There's a clever fix you can use to solve this problem.

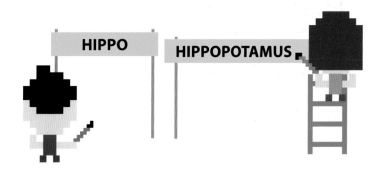

HIPPO   HIPPOPOTAMUS

1 Use an empty list

When you create the list that holds the clue, don't fill it with question marks – just leave the list empty. Make this change to the **clue** list.

```python
clue = []
```

There's nothing inside the brackets.

2 **Add a new loop**

To make the clue the correct length once the secret word has been selected, use this simple loop. It counts how many letters are in the word and adds a question mark for each letter.

```
clue = []

index = 0

while index < len(secret_word):

    clue.append('?')

    index = index + 1
```

The **append()** function simply adds an item to the end of the list.

Make the ending smarter

At the moment, the game doesn't end until you type out the word in full. Let's make the code smarter so the game ends when you guess the last letter.

At first all the letters are unknown.

1 **Make another variable**

First create a variable to keep count of how many letters are unknown. Add this code above the **update_clue** function.

```
unknown_letters = len(secret_word)
```

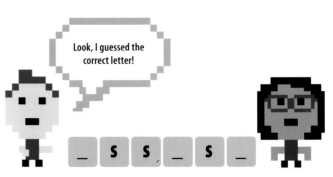

Look, I guessed the correct letter!

2 **Edit function**

Next change the **update_clue()** function as shown below. Each time the player guesses a letter correctly, the program will now take away the number of times that letter appears in the secret word from **unknown_letters**.

```
def update_clue(guessed_letter, secret_word, clue, unknown_letters):

    index = 0

    while index < len(secret_word):

        if guessed_letter == secret_word[index]:

            clue[index] = guessed_letter

            unknown_letters = unknown_letters - 1

        index = index + 1

    return unknown_letters
```

Add this new parameter to the **update_clue** function.

The code subtracts 1 from **unknown_letters** each time a guessed letter appears in the word.

This line makes the function return the number of unknown letters.

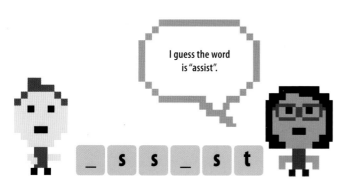

I guess the word is "assist".

_ s s _ s t

◁ **How it works**

Why do you have to update `unknown_letters` in the `update_clue ()` function? Why can't you just subtract 1 when you know that the guessed letter is in the secret word? This would work if each letter only appeared once in the secret word. But if the letter appears multiple times, it would make your count wrong. By updating the variable in the function, the code will subtract 1 from `unknown_letters` every time the letter appears in the secret word. This is because the function checks every letter in the secret word to see if it matches the guessed letter.

3 **Calling the function**

You'll also need to change the `update_clue ()` function to pass the `unknown_letters` variable and store the new value.

Hello, can you please connect me to the function?

```
if guess in secret_word:
    unknown_letters = update_clue(guess, secret_word, clue, unknown_letters)
else:
    print('Incorrect. You lose a life')
    lives = lives - 1
```

This passes the `unknown_letters` variable.

This line assigns the new value to the `unknown_letters` variable.

4 **Winning the game**

When `unknown_letters` reaches 0, the user has guessed the word correctly. Add this code at the end of the main loop. Now the game will automatically announce you as the winner when you've guessed all the letters.

Woohoo! I guessed the last letter!

```
    lives = lives - 1

if unknown_letters == 0:
    guessed_word_correctly = True
    break
```

The **break** statement exits the loop when the player guesses the correct word.

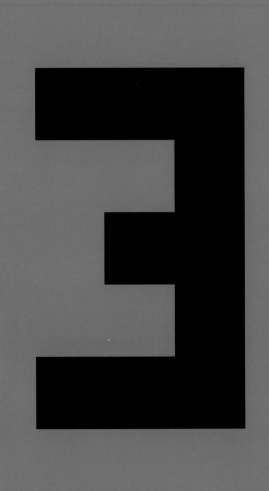

Turtle graphics

Robot Builder

Creating graphics in Python is easy. Python's Turtle Graphics module lets you move a robot "turtle" around the screen, drawing pictures with a pen as it goes. In this project, you'll program the turtle to build more robots – or at least pictures of robots!

What happens

When you run the program, Python's turtle sets off, scuttling around the screen as it draws a friendly robot. Watch as it assembles the robot piece by piece, using different colours.

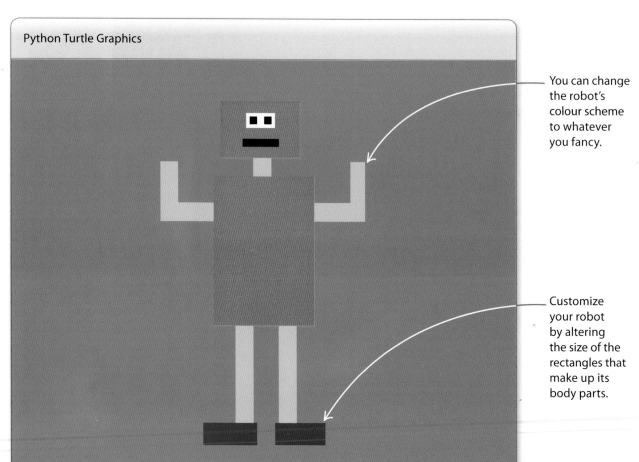

Python Turtle Graphics

You can change the robot's colour scheme to whatever you fancy.

Customize your robot by altering the size of the rectangles that make up its body parts.

How it works

You'll start by writing a function that draws rectangles. Then you'll put the rectangles together to build the robot. You can change the size and colour of the rectangles by altering the parameters you pass to the function. So you can have long, thin blocks for the legs, square ones for the eyes, and so on.

▽ **Don't call me turtle!**
Be careful never to name any of your Turtle programs "turtle.py". If you do that, Python will get really confused and give you lots of error messages.

I'm not a turtle! Don't call me that!

▽ **Drawing with the turtle**
The Turtle Graphics module allows you to control a pen-carrying robot turtle. By giving the turtle instructions on how it should move around the screen, you can draw different pictures and designs. You can also tell the turtle when to put the pen down and start drawing, or when to pull it up so it can move to a different part of the screen without leaving an untidy trail.

The turtle moves forward 100 pixels, turns left 90 degrees, then moves forwards 50 pixels.

```
t.forward(100)
t.left(90)
t.forward(50)
```

▽ **Robot Builder flowchart**
The flowchart shows how the code for this project fits together. First the program sets the background colour and how fast the turtle moves. Then it draws the robot one part at a time, starting from its feet and moving up to its head.

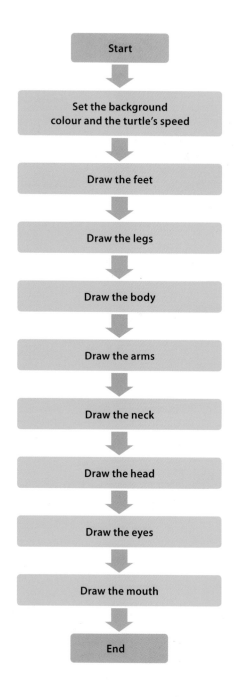

Start

Set the background colour and the turtle's speed

Draw the feet

Draw the legs

Draw the body

Draw the arms

Draw the neck

Draw the head

Draw the eyes

Draw the mouth

End

Drawing rectangles

Let's begin by importing the Turtle module and using it to create a function that draws rectangles.

1 **Create a new file**
Open IDLE and create a new file. Save it as "robot_builder.py".

Close
Save
Save As...
Save Copy As...

2 **Import the Turtle module**
Type this line at the top of your program. The command `import turtle as t` lets you use functions from the Turtle module without having to type "turtle" in full each time. It's like calling someone whose name is Benjamin "Ben" for short.

```
import turtle as t
```

This gives the Turtle module the nickname "t".

Like all programming languages, Python uses the US spelling "color".

3 **Create a rectangle function**
Now make the function to draw the blocks that you're going to use to build your robot. The function has three parameters: the length of the horizontal side; the length of the vertical side; and colour. You'll use a loop that draws one horizontal side and one vertical side each time it runs, and you'll make it run twice. Put this rectangle function under the code you added in Step 2.

```
def rectangle(horizontal, vertical, color):
    t.pendown()
    t.pensize(1)
    t.color(color)
    t.begin_fill()
    for counter in range(1, 3):
        t.forward(horizontal)
        t.right(90)
        t.forward(vertical)
        t.right(90)
    t.end_fill()
    t.penup()
```

Put the turtle's pen down to start drawing.

Using `range(1, 3)` makes the loop run twice.

Pull the turtle's pen back up to stop drawing.

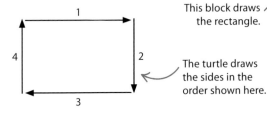

This block draws the rectangle.

The turtle draws the sides in the order shown here.

Turtle mode

You'll be using the turtle in its standard mode. This means the turtle starts off facing the right side of the screen. If you set the heading (another word for direction) to 0, it will face right. Setting the heading to 90 makes it point to the top of the screen, 180 points it to the left, and 270 makes it point to the bottom of the screen.

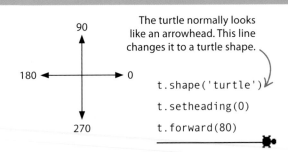

The turtle normally looks like an arrowhead. This line changes it to a turtle shape.

```
t.shape('turtle')
t.setheading(0)
t.forward(80)
```

Turtle speed

You can control how fast the turtle draws by using the `t.speed()` command to set its speed to one of these values: "slowest", "slow", "normal", "fast", and "fastest".

4 **Set the background**

Next get the turtle ready to start drawing, and set the background colour of the window. You need the turtle to start with its pen up so that it doesn't draw lines until you want it to. It will only begin to draw when it reaches the robot's feet (Step 5). Type the following code under the code you added in Step 3.

Pull the turtle's pen up.

Set the turtle's speed to slow.

```
t.penup()
t.speed('slow')
t.bgcolor('Dodger blue')
```

Make the background of the window "Dodger blue".

Building the robot

Now you're ready to start building the robot. You're going to make it piece by piece, starting with the feet and working your way up. The whole robot will be made using rectangles of different sizes and colours, each drawn from a different starting point in the Turtle window.

I'm going to build such a cool robot!

5 **Draw the feet**

You need to move the turtle to where you want to start drawing the first foot, and then use your rectangle function to draw it. You'll need to do the same for the second foot. Type these lines under the code you added in Step 4, then run the program to see your robot's feet appear.

This comment indicates which part of the robot you're drawing.

```
# feet
t.goto(-100, -150)
rectangle(50, 20, 'blue')
t.goto(-30, -150)
rectangle(50, 20, 'blue')
```

Move the turtle to position x = −100, y = −150.

Use the rectangle function to draw a blue rectangle 50 wide and 20 high.

Comments

You'll notice that there are several lines in this program that start with a # symbol. The words following the # are a comment, added to make the code easier for users to read and understand. Python knows that it should ignore them.

Turtle coordinates

Python will adjust the Turtle window to fit your screen, but let's use an example that's 400 pixels by 400 pixels. Python uses coordinates to identify all the places in the window where the turtle could be. This means that every place on the window can be found by using two numbers. The first number, the x coordinate, shows how far to the left or right of the centre the turtle is. The second number, the y coordinate, shows how far up or down from the centre it is. Coordinates are written in brackets, with the x coordinate first, like this: (x, y).

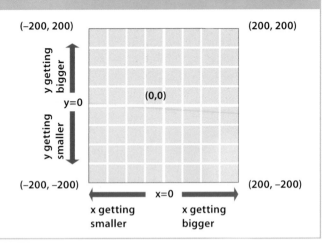

6 Draw the legs

The next bit of the program makes the turtle move to where it will start drawing the legs. Type these lines under the code you added in Step 5. Now run the code again.

The turtle moves to position x = –25, y = –50.

```
# legs
t.goto(-25, -50)
rectangle(15, 100, 'grey')
t.goto(-55, -50)
rectangle(-15, 100, 'grey')
```

Draw the left leg.

Draw the right leg.

7 Draw the body

Type this code under the code you added in Step 6. Run the program and you should see the body appear.

```
# body
t.goto(-90, 100)
rectangle(100, 150, 'red')
```

Draw a red rectangle 100 across and 150 down.

8 Draw the arms

Each arm is drawn in two parts: first the upper arm, from the robot's shoulder to its elbow; then the lower arm, from the elbow to the wrist. Type this below the code you added in Step 7, then run it to see the arms appear.

```
# arms
t.goto(-150, 70)
rectangle(60, 15, 'grey')       Upper right arm
t.goto(-150, 110)
rectangle(15, 40, 'grey')       Lower right arm

t.goto(10, 70)
rectangle(60, 15, 'grey')       Upper left arm
t.goto(55, 110)
rectangle(15, 40, 'grey')       Lower left arm
```

9 Draw the neck

Time to give your robot a neck. Type these neck-drawing commands below the code you added in Step 8.

```
# neck
t.goto(-50, 120)
rectangle(15, 20, 'grey')
```

10 Draw the head

Oops – you've drawn a headless robot! To give your poor robot a head, type these commands below the code you added in Step 9.

```
# head
t.goto(-85, 170)
rectangle(80, 50, 'red')
```

Don't forget to save your work.

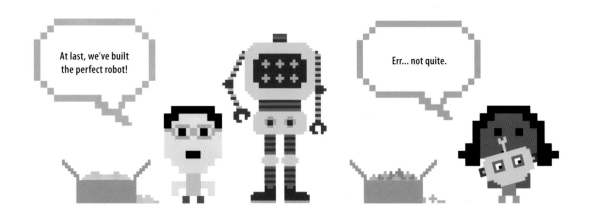

At last, we've built the perfect robot!

Err... not quite.

11 Draw the eyes

Let's add some eyes so that the robot can see where it's going. To do this, you'll draw a large white rectangle with two smaller squares inside it (for pupils). You don't have to write a new function to draw squares, since a square is a rectangle with all its sides the same length. Insert these commands under the code you added in Step 10.

```
# eyes
t.goto(-60, 160)
rectangle(30, 10, 'white')
t.goto(-55, 155)
rectangle(5, 5, 'black')
t.goto(-40, 155)
rectangle(5, 5, 'black')
```

Draw the white part of the eyes.

Draw the right pupil.

Draw the left pupil.

I've got eyes, but I still keep walking into things!!

12 Draw the mouth

Now give the robot a mouth. Type these commands under the code you added in Step 11.

```
# mouth
t.goto(-65, 135)
rectangle(40, 5, 'black')
```

13 Hide the turtle

Finally, hide the turtle so it doesn't look odd sitting on the robot's face. Type this line after the code you added in Step 12. Run the program to see the whole robot being built.

```
t.hideturtle()
```

This makes the turtle invisible.

I love to watch these robots being built!

I need a vacation!

Hacks and tweaks

Now your project is up and running, here are some ideas for modifying the code so you can customize the robots you build.

▽ **Change the colours**

The robot you've created is fairly colourful, but there's definitely room for improvement. You could change the code to build a robot that matches the colours of your room or your favourite football team's shirt, or create one that's totally multicoloured! On the right are some colours the turtle recognizes.

Lawn Green   Seashell   Blue

Purple   Light Blue   Yellow

Goldenrod   Hot Pink   Thistle

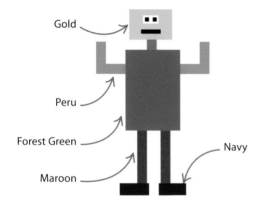

Gold

Peru

Forest Green

Maroon

Navy

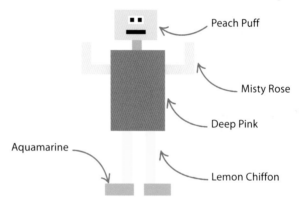

Peach Puff

Misty Rose

Deep Pink

Aquamarine

Lemon Chiffon

▷ **Change the face**

You can change the expression on the robot's face by rearranging its features. To give it wonky eyes and mouth, use the code on the right.

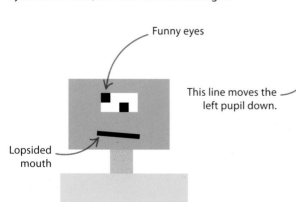

Funny eyes

Lopsided mouth

```
# eyes
t.goto(-60, 160)
rectangle(30, 10, 'white')
t.goto(-60, 160)
rectangle(5, 5, 'black')
t.goto(-45, 155)
rectangle(5, 5, 'black')

# mouth
t.goto(-65, 135)
t.right(5)
rectangle(40, 5, 'black')
```

This line moves the robot's right pupil, so it looks like the robot is rolling its eyes.

This line moves the left pupil down.

The turtle turns right slightly, which makes the mouth slope.

▷ **A helping hand**

Add this code to give your robot U-shaped gripping hands. You can reshape the hands to look like hooks, pincers, or anything else you like. Let your imagination run wild and create your own version!

```
# hands
t.goto(-155, 130)
rectangle(25, 25, 'green')
t.goto(-147, 130)
rectangle(10, 15, t.bgcolor())
t.goto(50, 130)
rectangle(25, 25, 'green')
t.goto(58, 130)
rectangle(10, 15, t.bgcolor())
```

Draw a green square for the main part of the hand.

Draw a small rectangle in the background colour to give the grip shape.

All-in-one arms

Drawing the arms in several parts makes it awkward to change their position or to add extra arms. In this hack, you'll write a function that draws an arm all in one go.

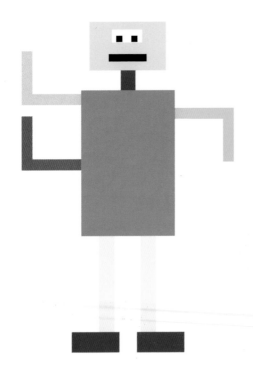

1 **Create an arm function**

First add this new function, which draws an arm shape and gives it colour.

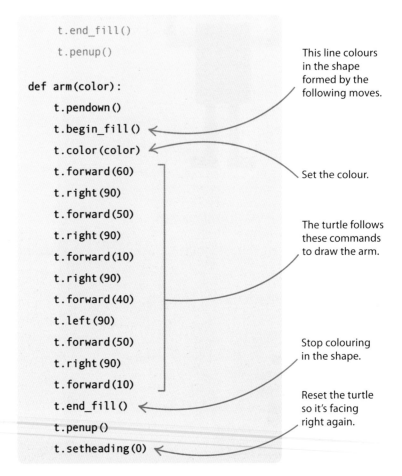

```
    t.end_fill()
    t.penup()

def arm(color):
    t.pendown()
    t.begin_fill()
    t.color(color)
    t.forward(60)
    t.right(90)
    t.forward(50)
    t.right(90)
    t.forward(10)
    t.right(90)
    t.forward(40)
    t.left(90)
    t.forward(50)
    t.right(90)
    t.forward(10)
    t.end_fill()
    t.penup()
    t.setheading(0)
```

This line colours in the shape formed by the following moves.

Set the colour.

The turtle follows these commands to draw the arm.

Stop colouring in the shape.

Reset the turtle so it's facing right again.

2 Add the arms

Next replace the code you originally had between the comment line **# arms** and the comment line **# neck** with the code shown here. It uses the arm function to draw three arms.

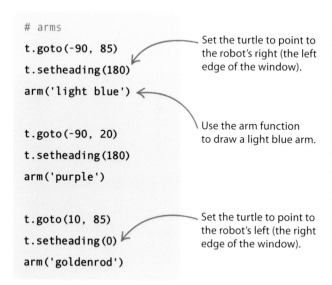

```
# arms
t.goto(-90, 85)
t.setheading(180)
arm('light blue')

t.goto(-90, 20)
t.setheading(180)
arm('purple')

t.goto(10, 85)
t.setheading(0)
arm('goldenrod')
```

Set the turtle to point to the robot's right (the left edge of the window).

Use the arm function to draw a light blue arm.

Set the turtle to point to the robot's left (the right edge of the window).

▽ Moving arms

Now that you can draw a whole arm in one go, you can change its position so the robot looks like it's scratching its head or maybe dancing a Highland Fling! To do this, use the **setheading()** function to change the direction the turtle is facing when it starts to draw the arm.

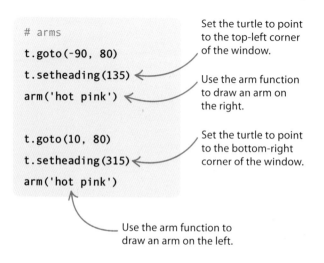

```
# arms
t.goto(-90, 80)
t.setheading(135)
arm('hot pink')

t.goto(10, 80)
t.setheading(315)
arm('hot pink')
```

Set the turtle to point to the top-left corner of the window.

Use the arm function to draw an arm on the right.

Set the turtle to point to the bottom-right corner of the window.

Use the arm function to draw an arm on the left.

Trial and error

When you're designing a robot or adding new features to an existing robot, it may take a bit of trial and error to get things just how you want them. If you add the lines **print(t.window_width())** and **print(t.window_height())** after the line **t.speed('slowest')**, Python will display the height and width of your Turtle window in the shell. Then mark out a grid of that size on graph-paper to help you to work out the coordinates of each body part.

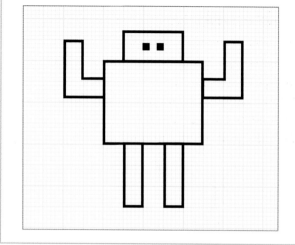

Can I have the next dance?

Kaleido-spiral

In the same way that simple lines of code can form a good program, simple shapes can form a complex picture. By combining shapes and colours through code, Kaleido-spiral will help you to create a masterpiece of digital art that's worthy of an art gallery!

What happens

Python's turtle draws circles on the screen, one after another. Each time a circle is drawn, the turtle changes the position, angle, colour, and size of the next circle it draws. A pattern gradually emerges.

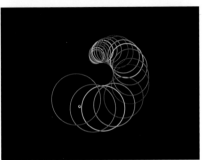

△ **Shifting spiral**
As the circles layer on top of each other, their shifting positions form a spiral snaking out from the centre.

Each circle is a different size and colour from the last.

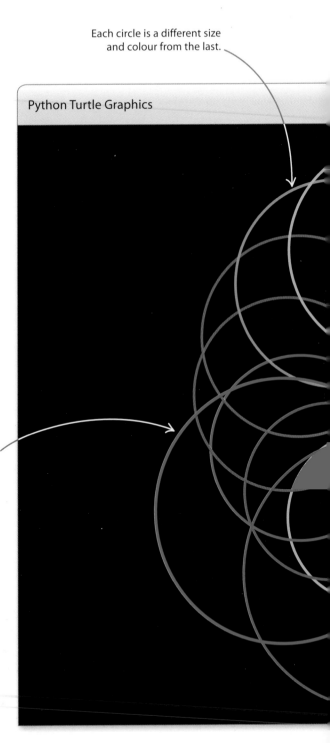

Python Turtle Graphics

The code hides the turtle, so it can't be seen while it draws the circles.

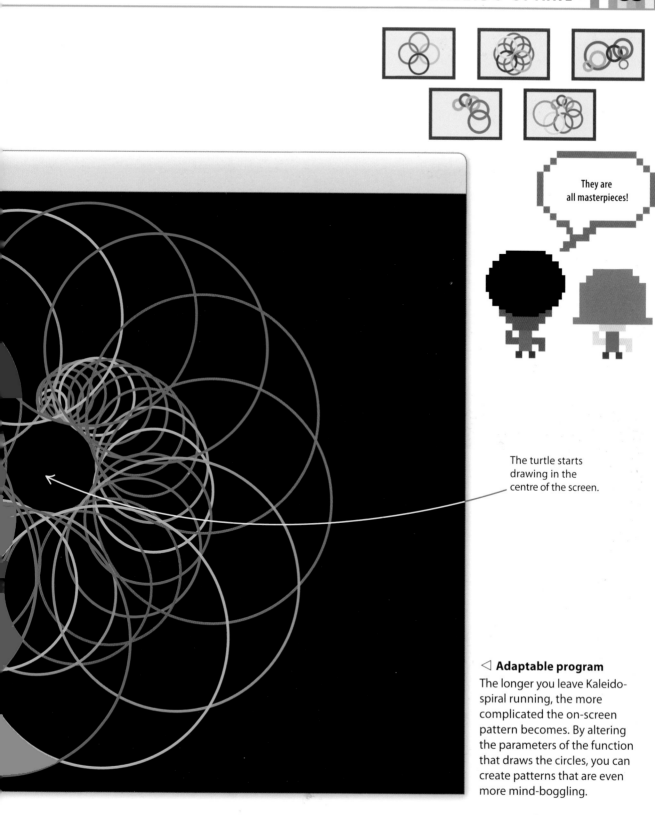

They are
all masterpieces!

The turtle starts
drawing in the
centre of the screen.

◁ **Adaptable program**
The longer you leave Kaleido-
spiral running, the more
complicated the on-screen
pattern becomes. By altering
the parameters of the function
that draws the circles, you can
create patterns that are even
more mind-boggling.

How it works

In this project, you'll use the **turtle** module and a clever looping technique to layer circles on top of each other in a spiral pattern. Every time a circle is drawn, the program slightly increases the parameters of the circle-drawing code. Each new circle is different from the last one drawn, making the pattern more interesting.

EXPERT TIPS

Cycling

To make the patterns colourful, this project uses a function called **cycle()** from the itertools module. The **cycle()** function allows you to cycle through a list of different colours over and over again. This makes it easy to use a different pen colour for each circle.

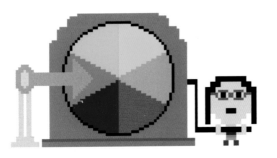

▽ **Kaleido-spiral flowchart**

The program sets some values that stay the same throughout, such as the turtle's speed, and then starts looping. The loop chooses a new pen colour, draws a circle, turns and moves the turtle, and then repeats itself. It stops when you quit the program.

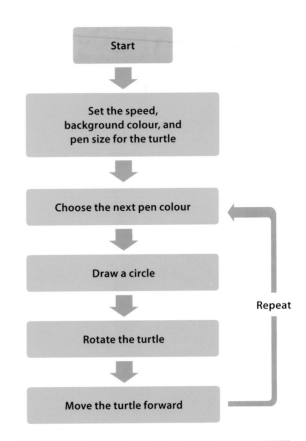

Start

Set the speed, background colour, and pen size for the turtle

Choose the next pen colour

Draw a circle

Rotate the turtle

Repeat

Move the turtle forward

Get drawing!

The first thing you'll draw on the screen is a simple circle. Next you'll repeat this circle, but with a slight change. Finally, you'll tweak the code to make the pattern more colourful and interesting.

1 **Create a new file**
Open IDLE and create a new file. Save it as "kaleido-spiral.py".

2 **Import turtle**
First you need to import the **turtle** module. This will be the main module you use. Type this line at the top of the program.

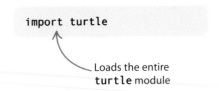

```
import turtle
```

Loads the entire **turtle** module

3 **Set up the turtle**
The code shown here calls functions in the **turtle** module to set the background colour, as well as the turtle's speed and size.

```
import turtle

turtle.bgcolor('black')
turtle.speed('fast')
turtle.pensize(4)
```

Background colour

The turtle's speed

The thickness of the turtle's trail

4 **Choose the pen colour, draw a circle**
Next set the colour of the turtle's trail and test the code by drawing a circle. Add these two lines to the end of your code and run the program.

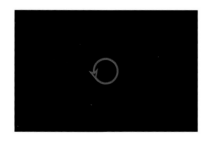

```
import turtle

turtle.bgcolor('black')
turtle.speed('fast')
turtle.pensize(4)

turtle.pencolor('red')
turtle.circle(30)
```

Pen colour

This tells the turtle to draw a circle.

5 **Draw more circles**
You should now see a single circle, but we need lots more. Here comes the clever bit. Put the commands to draw a red circle inside a function, but add a line so that the function calls itself. This trick, known as recursion, makes the function repeat. Remember, functions need to be defined before they're used, so you'll need to move the function above the line where it's called.

Hello, is that the function?

```
import turtle

def draw_circle(size):
    turtle.pencolor('red')
    turtle.circle(size)
    draw_circle(size)

turtle.bgcolor('black')
turtle.speed('fast')
turtle.pensize(4)
draw_circle(30)
```

This line uses the **size** parameter.

The function calls itself, which makes it repeat endlessly.

This line calls the function for the first time.

EXPERT TIPS

Recursion

When a function calls itself, this is known as recursion. It's another way of making a loop in your program. In most uses of recursion, the parameters of the function change each time the function is called. In Kaleido-spiral, for example, the size, angle, and position of the circle change whenever the function calls itself.

He's calling himself again!

6 **Test your code**
Run the program. You would see the turtle drawing the same circle over and over again. Don't worry – you'll fix that in the next step.

Wow!

WOW!

7 **Change the colour, increase the size**
To create more exciting patterns, make these changes to the code to increase the size of the circle and change its colour. This code uses the **cycle()** function, which takes a list of values as its parameter and returns a special type of list that you can cycle through endlessly using the **next()** function. Run the code again.

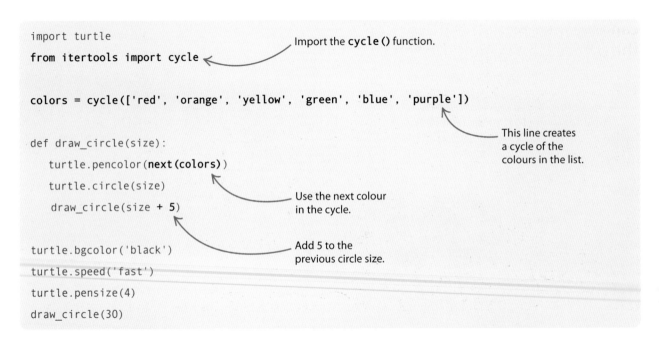

```
import turtle
from itertools import cycle

colors = cycle(['red', 'orange', 'yellow', 'green', 'blue', 'purple'])

def draw_circle(size):
    turtle.pencolor(next(colors))
    turtle.circle(size)
    draw_circle(size + 5)

turtle.bgcolor('black')
turtle.speed('fast')
turtle.pensize(4)
draw_circle(30)
```

Import the **cycle()** function.

This line creates a cycle of the colours in the list.

Use the next colour in the cycle.

Add 5 to the previous circle size.

8 **Improve the pattern**

Now that you've changed the colour and size of the circle, you can try a few more things to improve the pattern. Let's give it a zany twist by changing the angle and position at which each circle is drawn. Make the changes highlighted in the code below, then run the program and see what happens.

Don't forget to save your work.

```
def draw_circle(size, angle, shift):        Add these new parameters.
    turtle.pencolor(next(colors))
    turtle.circle(size)
    turtle.right(angle)                      The turtle turns clockwise.
    turtle.forward(shift)                    The turtle moves forward.
    draw_circle(size + 5, angle + 1, shift + 1)
                                             The angle and shift increase
turtle.bgcolor('black')                      with every circle drawn.
turtle.speed('fast')
turtle.pensize(4)
                                             Set the starting values
draw_circle(30, 0, 1)                        of the new parameters.
```

Hacks and tweaks

Once everything is working smoothly, you can play around with the code and make the patterns even more fantastic.

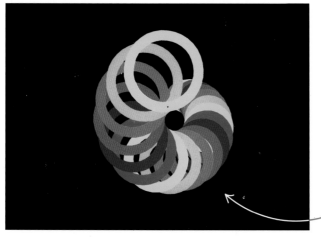

◁ **Chunky pen**

Try increasing the pen size and see what it does to your pattern. You originally set it to 4 with the code below. What would 40 look like?

```
turtle.pensize(40)
```

The circles become chunkier when you increase the pen size.

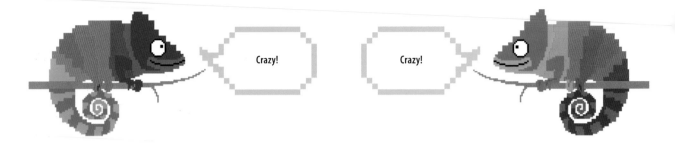

```
def draw_circle(size, angle, shift):
    turtle.bgcolor(next(colors))
    turtle.pencolor(next(colors))
    turtle.circle(size)
    turtle.right(angle)
    turtle.forward(shift)
    draw_circle(size + 5, angle + 1, shift + 1)


turtle.speed('fast')
turtle.pensize(4)
draw_circle(30, 0, 1)
```

The background colour is now set inside the loop.

◁ **Crazy colours**
What if you change the background colour on each loop, as well as the pen colour? It might give you some wild results! To get the background colour to change each time, move the line that sets it into the **draw_circle()** function. You'll also need to use the colour cycle to select a new colour on each loop.

▽ **Find new patterns**
The appearance of the pattern is determined by how much you add to the function's parameters each time it's called. Try adding more or less to the size, shift, and angle than you do at the moment, to find out how these changes affect the pattern.

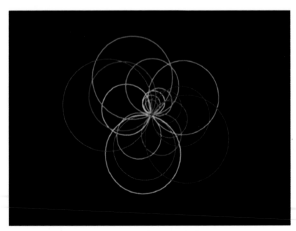

Size +10, angle +10, shift +1

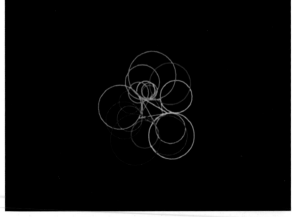

Size +5, angle −20, shift −10

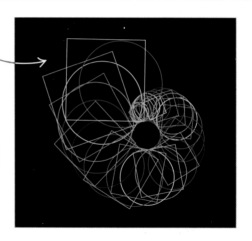

You can change the code to add different shapes.

I'll soon shift these shapes!

▽ **Shapeshifting**

How would the pattern look if the program could draw other shapes as well as circles? Adding a square every other time might create an interesting pattern. Here's some code to help you out. Be careful – the name of the function has changed!

```python
import turtle
from itertools import cycle


colors = cycle(['red', 'orange', 'yellow', 'green', 'blue', 'purple'])


def draw_shape(size, angle, shift, shape):
    turtle.pencolor(next(colors))
    next_shape = ''
    if shape == 'circle':
        turtle.circle(size)
        next_shape = 'square'
    elif shape == 'square':
        for i in range(4):
            turtle.forward(size * 2)
            turtle.left(90)
        next_shape = 'circle'
    turtle.right(angle)
    turtle.forward(shift)
    draw_shape(size + 5, angle + 1, shift + 1, next_shape)

turtle.bgcolor('black')
turtle.speed('fast')
turtle.pensize(4)
draw_shape(30, 0, 1, 'circle')
```

Add a new parameter, **shape**.

The loop runs 4 times, once for each side of the square.

The turtle rotates.

The turtle moves forward.

This makes the turtle alternate between circles and squares.

The first shape is a circle.

Starry Night

Fill your screen with beautiful stars! This project uses Python's `turtle` module to draw star shapes. Random numbers scatter the stars over the screen and vary their colour, size, and shape.

A new Turtle Graphics window opens when you run the program.

The turtle draws the stars one by one.

Python Turtle Graphics

What happens

First a night-time sky is drawn, then a single star appears in the sky. As the program continues, the sky begins to fill with more and more stars in a wide range of different styles. The longer you leave the program running, the more fantastic and colourful the sky becomes.

Making colours

Pictures and graphics on a computer screen are made up of tiny dots called pixels, which can give out red, green, and blue light. By mixing these colours together you can make any colour imaginable. In this project, the colour of each star is stored as three numbers. The numbers represent the amounts of red, green, and blue light that are combined to give the final colour.

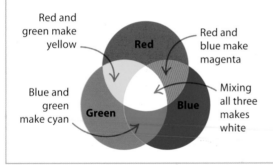

Red and green make yellow

Red and blue make magenta

Blue and green make cyan

Mixing all three makes white

Red

Green   Blue

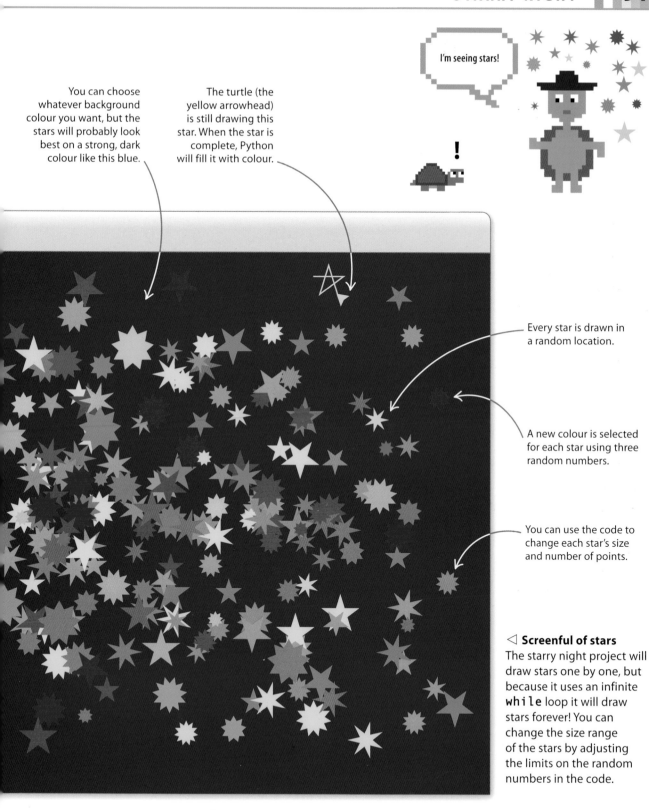

I'm seeing stars!

You can choose whatever background colour you want, but the stars will probably look best on a strong, dark colour like this blue.

The turtle (the yellow arrowhead) is still drawing this star. When the star is complete, Python will fill it with colour.

Every star is drawn in a random location.

A new colour is selected for each star using three random numbers.

You can use the code to change each star's size and number of points.

◁ **Screenful of stars**
The starry night project will draw stars one by one, but because it uses an infinite `while` loop it will draw stars forever! You can change the size range of the stars by adjusting the limits on the random numbers in the code.

How it works

The code for this project draws star shapes at random locations in a Turtle Graphics window. You'll write Python code to create a function that can draw a single star. Then you'll make a loop that repeats it over and over, drawing lots of different stars all over the screen.

201, 202, 203...
Oh, I think I missed one!

Have you tried using a loop?

◁ **Counting stars**
On a clear night there are around 4,500 stars visible in the sky. To get your program to draw that many stars, you'd need to leave it running for over 3 hours!

▽ **Starry Night flowchart**
The flowchart is quite simple, with no questions to be asked or decisions to be made. Once the turtle has drawn the first star, the program loops back and repeats the star-drawing steps nonstop until you quit.

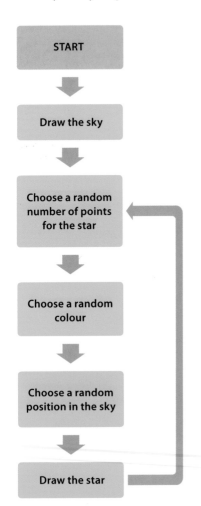

START

↓

Draw the sky

↓

Choose a random number of points for the star

↓

Choose a random colour

↓

Choose a random position in the sky

↓

Draw the star

Draw a star

Before you create your function, you need to find out how to draw a star in Turtle. When you've mastered that, you'll be able to build the rest of the code for the project.

1 **Create a new file**
Open IDLE. Go to the File menu, then select New File. Save the file as "starry_night.py".

2 **Import turtle**
Type this line into the editor window that appears. It loads the turtle module, ready for you to start drawing your star.

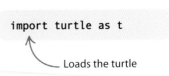

```
import turtle as t
```
↑
Loads the turtle

3 **Write some instructions**
Now add this code beneath the command to import turtle. It creates variables that set the size and shape of the star. It also tells the turtle how to move over the window to draw the star.

```
import turtle as t

size = 300
points = 5
angle = 144

for i in range(points):
    t.forward(size)
    t.right(angle)
```

These are the instructions for the size and shape of the star.

This is the angle formed by each star point, shown in degrees.

This **for** loop makes the turtle repeat the same movement for each point of the star.

4 **Draw a test star**
From the IDLE menu, select Run and then "Run Module" to test the project. The Turtle Graphics window will appear (it might be behind another window) and you'll see the turtle arrow begin to draw your star.

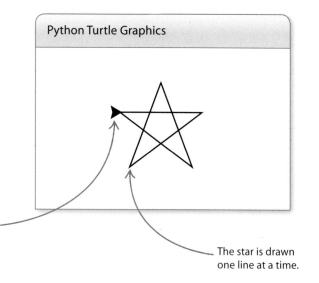

Python Turtle Graphics

The turtle arrow moves in the window, drawing lines as it goes.

The star is drawn one line at a time.

Don't forget to save your work.

5 **Add an angle calculator**
It would be good to be able to draw stars with different numbers of points. Make this change to the code. It will calculate the angle of the turns that the turtle needs to make to draw a star with however many points you choose.

```
import turtle as t

size = 300
points = 5
angle = 180 - (180 / points)

for i in range(points):
    t.forward(size)
    t.right(angle)
```

The angle depends on the number of points the star has.

6 Colour it!

You've drawn a nice, neat star, but it looks rather dull at the moment. Let's add some colour to make it more attractive. Change the code as shown on the right to paint your star yellow.

7 Run the project

The turtle should draw a yellow star. See if you can change the star's colour by editing the code.

```
import turtle as t

size = 300
points = 5
angle = 180 - (180 / points)


t.color('yellow')
t.begin_fill()
  for i in range(points):
      t.forward(size)
      t.right(angle)


t.end_fill()
```

This sets the star's colour to yellow.

This fills the star with colour.

That's bright!

8 Draw different stars

Try changing the number after the equals sign in the variable **points** and you'll see that you can draw different stars. Note that the code only works for stars with odd numbers of points. Even numbers will mess things up.

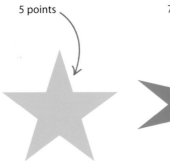

5 points

7 points

11 points

∙ ∙ EXPERT TIPS

Holey stars

On some computers your star might look slightly different or even have a hole in the middle. The appearance of Python's Turtle Graphics can vary depending on the type of computer you use, but this doesn't mean that your code is wrong.

Don't forget to save your work.

Starry sky

The next steps will wrap up your star as a Python function. You'll then be able to use that function to draw a sky that's teeming with stars.

I think I just spotted the Crab Nebula!

The **draw_star()** function uses five parameters to define the shape, size, colour, and position of the star.

9 **Create the star function**
Edit the code as shown here. It replaces nearly all of your existing code with a new version. The large block wraps up all the star-drawing instructions and keeps them neatly together as a function. You can now use this function to draw a star in your main code with a single line of Python, **draw_star()**.

```python
import turtle as t


def draw_star(points, size, col, x, y):
    t.penup()
    t.goto(x, y)
    t.pendown()
    angle = 180 - (180 / points)
    t.color(col)
    t.begin_fill()
    for i in range(points):
        t.forward(size)
        t.right(angle)
    t.end_fill()


# Main code
t.Screen().bgcolor('dark blue')
draw_star(5, 50, 'yellow', 0, 0)
```

The x and y coordinates set the position of the star on the screen.

This sets the background colour to dark blue.

This "comment" line starting with a hash symbol (#) isn't part of the code run by Python. It's like a label to help you understand the program.

This line calls (runs) the function.

The turtle draws a yellow, five-pointed star, size 50, in the centre the window.

10 **Run the project**
The turtle should draw a single yellow star on a blue background.

Python Turtle Graphics

• • • REMEMBER

Comments

Programmers often put comments in their code to remind them what different parts of a program do or to explain a tricky part of a project. A comment must start with a #. Python ignores anything you type on the same line after the # and doesn't treat it as part of the code. Writing comments in your own projects (such as the line **# Main code** shown above) can be really helpful when you go back to look at a program after leaving it for a while.

11 **Add random numbers**
Now mix things up by adding some random numbers to your code. Type this line under the line that imports Turtle. It brings in the **randint ()** and **random ()** functions from Python's **random** module.

```
import turtle as t

from random import randint, random


def draw_star(points, size, col, x, y):
```

12 **Create a loop**
Make this change to the **#Main code** section. It adds a **while** loop that continually randomizes the parameters used to set the stars' size, shape, colour, and position.

The **ranPts** line sets the limit for the number of points on the star to be an odd number between 5 and 11.

This line also changes. When it calls the **draw_star ()** function, it will now use the random variables in the **while** loop.

```
# Main code
t.Screen().bgcolor('dark blue')


while True:
    ranPts = randint(2, 5) * 2 + 1
    ranSize = randint(10, 50)
    ranCol = (random(), random(), random())
    ranX = randint(-350, 300)
    ranY = randint(-250, 250)


    draw_star(ranPts, ranSize, ranCol, ranX, ranY)
```

13 **Run the project again**
The window should slowly fill up as the turtle draws star after star in a range of colours, shapes, and sizes.

Python Turtle Graphics

The turtle draws stars randomly.

Wow!

Hacks and tweaks

You can now create stars on demand. Why not try using the `draw_star()` code in your own projects. Here are just a few ideas.

It's all in the mouse control!

▷ **Click for the stars**
Instead of letting the turtle draw stars randomly, try using the `turtle.onScreenClick()` function to draw a star wherever you click with the mouse.

△ **Change your stars**
To change how varied your stars look, alter the numbers in the brackets of the `ranPts` and `ranSize` variables in the `while` loop.

▽ **Speed up the turtle**
You can change how fast the turtle draws the stars by creating a `speed()` function. Just add `t.speed(0)` at the start of the main code to give the turtle more zip. You can see all the turtle package's functions in Python's "Help" section.

▽ **Design a constellation**
A constellation is a pattern of stars in the night sky. Try creating a list of (x, y) positions for stars in a constellation of your own design. Then use a `for` loop to draw the stars at those locations.

I'm quick on the draw!

We're lost! You'll have to get out and ask the way...

Try to add some rings around your planets.

Has anyone seen a planet around here?

▷ **Draw some planets**
Investigate the `turtle.circle()` function and see if you can use it to make some planet-drawing code. Here's some code to get you started.

```
def draw_planet(col, x, y):
    t.penup()
    t.goto(x, y)
    t.pendown()
    t.color(col)
    t.begin_fill()
    t.circle(50)
    t.end_fill()
```

Mutant Rainbow

You can program Python's turtle to draw all sorts of patterns and designs. But watch out! Looks like the turtle in this project has gone a bit wild – you wouldn't see rainbows like this in the sky!

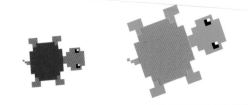

What happens

The program will ask you to choose the length and thickness of the line that the turtle paints. The turtle then scurries around the screen until you stop the program, painting coloured lines as it goes. The type of pattern it makes will change, depending on the length and thickness of the lines.

The turtle has a "pen" that paints lines as the turtle moves over the window.

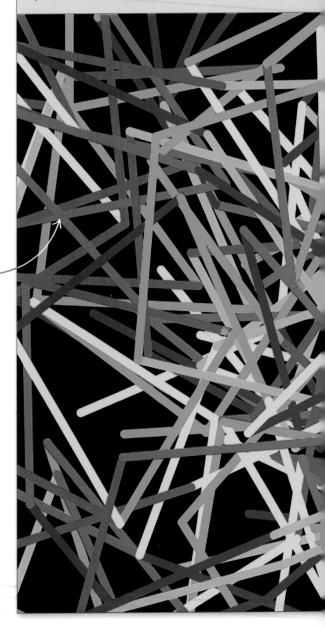

Python Turtle Graphics

. . . **EXPERT TIPS**

Which colour next?

In Mutant Rainbow, you'll use the `choice()` function from Python's random library to pick a colour when you tell the turtle to draw a line. This means that you can't really predict which colour the turtle will use each time.

```
t.pencolor(random.choice(pen_colors))
```

The turtle chooses from the six colours you put in the list **pen_colors**.

It's a rainbow of possibilities!

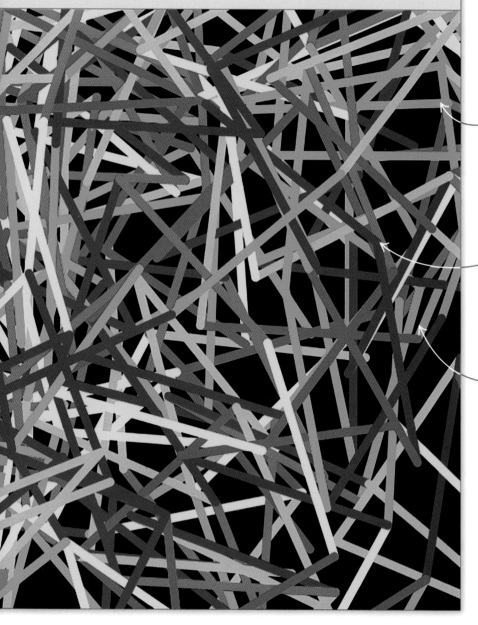

The turtle can paint in green, red, orange, yellow, blue, and purple.

The turtle can make right-hand turns between 0 and 180 degrees.

You can make the turtle paint long, medium, or short lines using the `line_length()` function.

◁ **A display of colours**
Because this program uses an infinite `while` loop, the turtle keeps drawing until you close its window. You can not only change the colour, width, and length of the lines, but also the shape, colour, and speed of the turtle itself.

How it works

Every pattern in this project is different because the program tells the turtle to face a random new direction before painting each line. The colour for each line is also chosen at random from a list of possible colours you've coded. So you can never predict exactly what the turtle will do!

Long, thick

Medium, thin

Short, superthick

▽ **Mutant Rainbow flowchart**

The program uses an infinite loop that continues to paint coloured lines for as long as the program is running. Only when you close the window will the turtle stop its mazy wanderings.

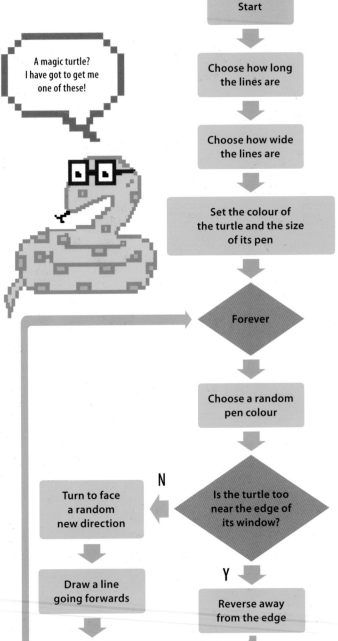

◁ **Runaway turtle!**
Given complete freedom to roam, the turtle tends to wander out of the window. As you put the program together, you'll write some code to check on the turtle's position and stop it from straying too far. Otherwise, this will turn into a vanishing turtle project!

Getting started

Start by setting up and saving a new file, importing the modules that the program will need, and making a couple of useful functions to get user input.

1 Create new files
Open IDLE and create a new file. Save it as "rainbow.py".

2 Add the modules
Type these two lines at the top of your file to import the Turtle module and the random module. Remember to use **import turtle as t**, so that you don't have to type the word "turtle" every time you want to use a function from the Turtle module. You can just call it **t**.

```python
import random
import turtle as t
```

3 Assign line length
Next make a function that will let the user decide whether the turtle paints long, medium, or short lines. You won't use it until Step 4, but this will get the program ready for when you need it. Type this bit of code beneath the code in Step 1.

```python
import turtle as t


def get_line_length():
    choice = input('Enter line length (long, medium, short): ')
    if choice == 'long':
        line_length = 250
    elif choice == 'medium':
        line_length = 200
    else:
        line_length = 100
    return line_length
```

This asks the user to choose how long the line is.

For a short line, set **line_length** to 100.

This command passes **line_length** back to the code that called this function.

4 Define thickness

In this step, you'll create a function that will let the user choose whether the turtle paints superthick, thick, or thin lines. Like the `get_line_length()` function, you won't use it until Step 5. Type the code shown here, under the code you added in Step 3.

If short lines are chosen, this sets `line_width` to 10.

```
return line_length

def get_line_width():
    choice = input('Enter line width (superthick, thick, thin): ')
    if choice == 'superthick':
        line_width = 40
    elif choice == 'thick':
        line_width = 25
    else:
        line_width = 10
    return line_width
```

This asks the user to choose how thick the line is.

This command passes `line_width` back to the code that used this function.

5 Use the functions

Now you've built the two functions, you can use them to get the user's choices for line length and width. Type these lines at the end of your code, then save your work.

```
        return line_width

line_length = get_line_length()
line_width = get_line_width()
```

6 Test the program

Run the code to see the new functions in action in the shell. They'll ask you to select the length and width of the lines.

User input

```
Enter line length (long, medium, short): long
Enter line width (superthick, thick, thin): thin
```

Summon the turtle!

It's time to write the code that will create a graphics window and bring in the turtle to do the drawing.

7 Open a window

Type the lines shown here under the code you added in Step 5. This code defines the background colour of the window, the shape, colour, and speed of the turtle, as well as the width of the pen the turtle will use to draw lines.

This sets the pen's width to the user's choice.

```
line_width = get_line_width()

t.shape('turtle')
t.fillcolor('green')
t.bgcolor('black')
t.speed('fastest')
t.pensize(line_width)
```

The turtle's standard shape is an arrowhead. This changes it to a turtle shape.

This makes the turtle green.

This sets the background to black.

This sets the turtle's speed.

8 **Run the project**
If you run the code once more, a window will appear after you've entered the line sizes in the shell window. You will now see the turtle. Take a good look at it, because it won't be sitting still for too long!

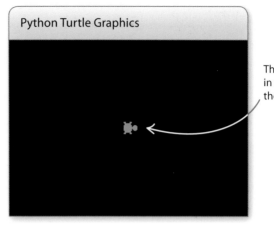

Python Turtle Graphics

The turtle starts in the middle of the window.

9 **Keep inside the limits!**
To stop the turtle from straying, let's set a boundary 100 steps in from the edges of the window. Create this function to check whether or not the turtle is inside the boundary. Type the code shown here under the code in Step 4 and above the code in Step 5.

```
    return line_width


def inside_window():
    left_limit = (-t.window_width() / 2) + 100
    right_limit = (t.window_width() / 2) - 100
    top_limit = (t.window_height() / 2) - 100
    bottom_limit = (-t.window_height() / 2) + 100
    (x, y) = t.pos()
    inside = left_limit < x < right_limit and bottom_limit < y < top_limit
    return inside

line_length = get_line_length()
```

This is 100 steps to the right of the left edge.

100 steps from the right edge

100 steps from the top

100 steps from the bottom

This sets **inside** to **True** if the turtle is inside the limits and **False** if it isn't.

With this line, the program gets the turtle's current x and y coordinates.

This command passes **inside** back to the code that used this function.

▷ **How it works**
The code checks if the turtle's x coordinate is between the right and left limits, and if its y coordinate is between the top and bottom limits.

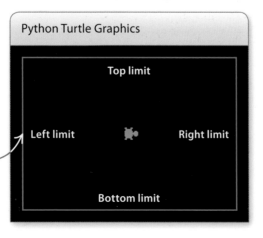

Python Turtle Graphics

Top limit

Left limit

Right limit

Bottom limit

The blue square is shown here to tell you where the limits are set – it won't be visible on your screen.

Don't forget to save your work.

Move that turtle!

Now you're ready to write the function that gets your turtle moving. The last bit of the code will be a `while` loop that sets the turtle off drawing mutant rainbows!

Move along now, please!

10 **Mutant line**

Add this code below the code you typed in Step 9, and above the code you typed in Step 5. This function makes the turtle turn and move forwards in a new direction, drawing a single line of random colour as it goes. Your main program will use it over and over again to draw mutant rainbows. If the turtle strays beyond the limits you set in Step 9, this function will bring it back.

The different colours the pen can use are stored in a list.

Use a backslash character if you need to split a long line of code over two lines.

▷ **How it works**

The code calls the `inside_window()` function to see if the turtle is within the window limits. If it is, the turtle turns right by a random amount between 0 degrees (doesn't turn at all) and 180 degrees (faces the opposite direction), then moves off again. If it has gone too far from the limit, it moves backwards.

```
return inside

def move_turtle(line_length):
    pen_colors = ['red', 'orange', 'yellow', 'green', \
                  'blue', 'purple']
    t.pencolor(random.choice(pen_colors))
    if inside_window():
        angle = random.randint(0, 180)
        t.right(angle)
        t.forward(line_length)
    else:
        t.backward(line_length)


line_length = get_line_length()
```

The pen chooses a colour at random.

This checks if the turtle is inside the set limits.

The turtle turns right by the random angle.

If the turtle is outside the limits, it moves backwards.

This chooses a random angle between 0 and 180 degrees.

11 **Go, Turtle, Go!**

Finally, add the code that will actually start your turtle drawing. Type these two lines right at the bottom of your code, under the commands you added in Step 7. Then save and run the code to see your first mutant rainbow!

This line starts an infinite loop to make the turtle draw nonstop.

The turtle moves forward in `line_length` steps.

```
t.speed('fastest')
t.pensize(line_width)


while True:
    move_turtle(line_length)
```

The turtle draws one line.

Hacks and tweaks

Are your rainbows mutant enough? No? Here are some ideas you could try to make them even more bizarre!

▽ **Colour surprise!**

In Python, colours can also be described by using RGB values – this stands for red, green, blue. Choosing values at random for the amounts of red, green, and blue in a colour means the colour itself will be completely random. Try replacing the code in the `move_turtle()` function with some new code that uses RGB values instead of colour names. Now run the code to see what colours appear!

Replace these two lines with...

```python
pen_colors = ['red', 'orange', 'yellow', 'green', 'blue', 'purple']
t.pencolor(random.choice(pen_colors))
```

...these five lines.

```python
t.colormode(255)
red = random.randint(0, 255)
blue = random.randint(0, 255)
green = random.randint(0, 255)
t.pencolor(red, green, blue)
```

⬛ ⬛ ▪ EXPERT TIPS

RGB colours

The turtle colour "blue" is (0, 0, 255) in RGB values, as it's made up of the maximum amount of blue, with no red or green. If you want to use RGB values for the turtle's pen colour, you need to let Python know by using the command `t.colormode(255)`, or it will expect a string and give you an error.

This number shows the amount of red in the colour (between 0 and 255).

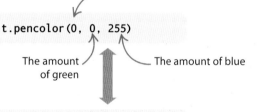

```python
t.pencolor(0, 0, 255)
```

The amount of green

The amount of blue

```python
t.pencolor('blue')
```

▽ **Mix up the lines**

Don't just stick to one width for the line – draw even more scrambled rainbows with this hack! The lines will change at random from really thin to superthick and all widths in between. Add this code to the `move_turtle()` function after you set `t.pencolor`.

```python
t.pensize(random.randint(1,40))
```

▽ **Stamp the turtle!**

"Rivet" the lines of your rainbows together by using the Turtle module's **stamp()** function to add a turtle's picture to the beginning of each line. (You could also write a function to draw a line entirely made up of stamped turtles and use it instead of **t.forward** and **t.backward**.) Add these new lines of code to the **move_turtle()** function, after the pen commands, to start riveting.

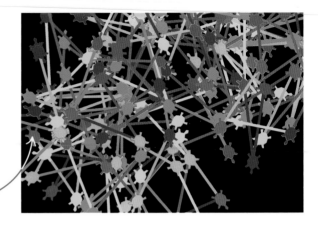

The turtle stamps look like rivets holding the lines together.

```
def move_turtle(line_length):
    pen_colors = ['red', 'orange', 'yellow', 'green', 'blue', 'purple']
    t.pencolor(random.choice(pen_colors))
    t.fillcolor(random.choice(pen_colors))
    t.shapesize(3,3,1)
    t.stamp()
    if inside_window():
```

This sets the colour of the turtle to a random colour.

Type this to stamp a turtle picture on the screen.

This makes the turtle three times bigger than usual.

Big or small turns?

You can add a prompt that allows the user to decide the angle of the turns the turtle makes. They can be wide, square, or narrow. Follow these steps to see how this changes the patterns.

1 **Make a function**

Create a function that lets the user choose the size of a turn. Add this above the **get_line_length()** function you added in Step 3 of the main project.

Type this to get the user's choice of turn angle.

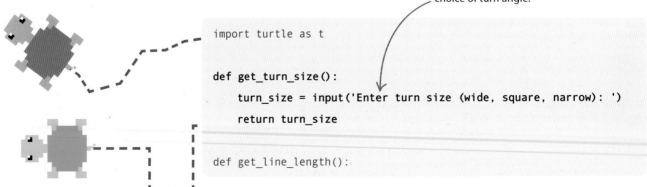

```
import turtle as t

def get_turn_size():
    turn_size = input('Enter turn size (wide, square, narrow): ')
    return turn_size


def get_line_length():
```

2 Different moves

Replace the **move_turtle()** function with the new version shown here. It adds **turn_size** to the values you pass to the function when you use it. It also replaces the line **angle = random. randint (0, 180)** with code that chooses different degrees to turn depending on the value of **turn_size**.

Square turns are between 80 and 90 degrees.

Narrow turns are between 20 and 40 degrees.

Wide turns are between 120 and 150 degrees

```python
def move_turtle(line_length, turn_size):
    pen_colors = ['red', 'orange', 'yellow', 'green', \
'blue', 'purple']
    t.pencolor(random.choice(pen_colors))
    if inside_window():
        if turn_size == 'wide':
            angle = random.randint(120, 150)
        elif turn_size == 'square':
            angle = random.randint(80, 90)
        else:
            angle = random.randint(20, 40)
        t.right(angle)
        t.forward(line_length)
    else:
        t.backward(line_length)
```

3 User input

Next add a line to the main part of the program to use the **get_turn_size()** function to get the player's choice of turn size.

```python
line_length = get_line length()
line_width = get_line_width()
turn_size = get_turn_size()
```

4 Main program

Finally change the line where you use the **move_turtle()** function to include **turn_size**.

```python
while True:
        move_turtle(line_length, turn_size)
```

Short, thick, narrow

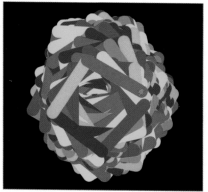

Medium, superthick, square

Long, thin, wide

Playful
apps

Countdown Calendar

When you're looking forward to an exciting event, it helps to know how much longer you have to wait. In this project, you'll use Python's `Tkinter` module to build a handy program that counts down to the big day.

Hooray! It's 0 days until my birthday!

What happens

When you run the program it shows a list of future events and tells you how many days there are until each one. Run it again the next day and you'll see that it has subtracted one day from each of the "days until" figures. Fill it with the dates of your forthcoming adventures and you'll never miss an important day – or a homework deadline – again!

Give your calendar a personalized title.

```
tk

My Countdown Calendar ←

It is 20 days until Halloween
It is 51 days until Spanish Test
It is 132 days until School Trip
It is 92 days until My Birthday
```

A small window pops up when you run the program, with each event on a separate line.

How it works

The program learns about the important events by reading information from a text file – this is called "file input". The text file contains the name and date of each event. The code calculates the number of days from today until each event using Python's `datetime` module. It displays the results in a window created by Python's `Tkinter` module.

▷ Using Tkinter

The `Tkinter` module is a set of tools that Python programmers use for displaying graphics and getting input from users. Instead of showing output in the shell, `Tkinter` can display results in a separate window that you're able to design and style yourself.

LINGO

Graphical user interface

A GUI (graphical user interface) is the visible part of a program you interact with, such as the system of icons and menus on a smartphone. Python's `Tkinter` module allows you to build a GUI by using what we call widgets – packages of ready-made code that create pop-up windows, buttons, sliders, menus and so on.

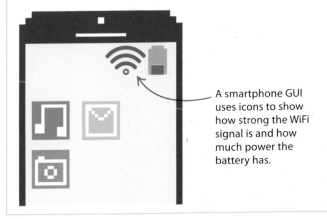

A smartphone GUI uses icons to show how strong the WiFi signal is and how much power the battery has.

▽ Countdown Calendar flowchart

In this project, the list of important events is created separately from the code as a text file. The program begins by reading in all the events from this file. Once all the days have been calculated and displayed, the program ends.

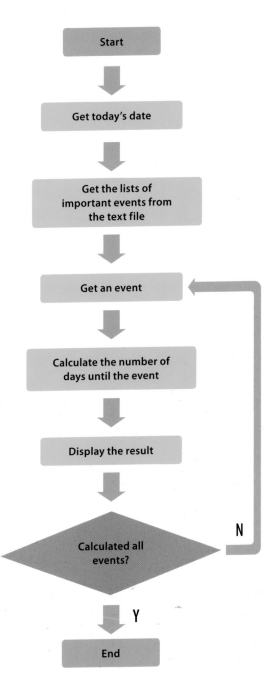

Making and reading the text file

All the information for your Countdown Calendar must be stored in a text file. You can create it using IDLE.

1 Create a new file

Open a new IDLE file, then type in a few upcoming events that are important to you. Put each event on a separate line and type a comma between the event and its date. Make sure there is no space between the comma and the event date.

Type the date as day/month/year.

events.txt

```
Halloween,31/10/17
Spanish Test,01/12/17
School Trip,20/02/18
My Birthday,11/01/18
```

The name of the event comes first.

So many events, so little time.

2 Save it as a text file

Next save the file as a text file. Click the File menu, choose Save As, and call the file "events.txt". Now you're ready to start coding the Python program.

```
Close
Save
Save As...
Save Copy As...
```

3 Open a new Python file

You now need to create a new file for the code. Save it as "countdown_calendar.py" and make sure it's in the same folder as your "events.txt" file.

4 Set up the modules

This project needs two modules: **Tkinter** and **datetime**. **Tkinter** will be used to build a simple GUI, while **datetime** will make it easy to do calculations using dates. Import them by typing these two lines at the top of your new program.

```
from tkinter import Tk, Canvas
from datetime import date, datetime
```

Import the **Tkinter** and **datetime** modules.

5 **Create the canvas**
Now add the follwoing code beneath the lines you added in Step 3. The first line uses **Tkinter**'s **root** widget to create a window. The second line uses the **Canvas** widget to add a blank rectangle (a canvas) that you can add text and graphics to.

Canvas

In **Tkinter**, the canvas is an area, usually a rectangle, where you can place different shapes, graphics, text, or images that the user can look at or interact with. Think of it like an artist's canvas – except you're using code to create things rather than a paintbrush!

This command packs the canvas into the **Tkinter** window.

Create a **Tkinter** window.

Create a canvas called **c** that is 800 pixels wide by 800 pixels high.

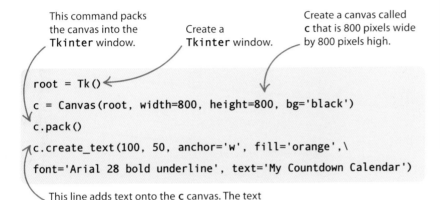

```
root = Tk()
c = Canvas(root, width=800, height=800, bg='black')
c.pack()
c.create_text(100, 50, anchor='w', fill='orange',\
font='Arial 28 bold underline', text='My Countdown Calendar')
```

This line adds text onto the **c** canvas. The text starts at x = 100, y = 50. The starting coordinate is at the left (west) of the text.

6 **Run the code**
Now try running the code. You'll see a window appear with the title of the program. If it doesn't work, remember to read any error messages and go through your code carefully to spot possible mistakes.

I'll soon track down those errors!

tk

My Countdown Calendar

You can change the colour by altering the **c.create_text()** line in the code.

7 **Read the text file**
Next create a function that will read and store all the events from the text file. At the top of your code, after importing the module, create a new function called **get_events**. Inside the function is an empty list that will store the events when the file has been read.

```
from datetime import date, datetime
def get_events():
    list_events = []
root = Tk()
```

Create an empty list called **list_events**.

8 Open the text file

This next bit of code will open the file called events.txt so the program can read it. Type in this line underneath your code from Step 7.

```
def get_events():
    list_events = []
    with open('events.txt') as file:
```

This line opens the text file.

9 Start a loop

Now add a **for** loop to bring information from the text file into your program. The loop will be run for every line in the events.txt file.

```
def get_events():
    list_events = []
    with open('events.txt') as file:
        for line in file:
```

Run the loop for each line in the text file.

10 Remove the invisible character

When you typed information into the text file in Step 1, you pressed the enter/return key at the end of each line. This added an invisible "newline" character at the end of every line. Although you can't see this character, Python can. Add this line of code, which tells Python to ignore these invisible characters when it reads the text file.

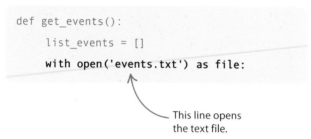

```
with open('events.txt') as file:
    for line in file:
        line = line.rstrip('\n')
```

Remove the newline character from each line.

The newline character is represented as ('\n') in Python.

11 Store the event details

At this point, the variable called **line** holds the information about each event as a string, such as **Halloween,31/10/2017**. Use the **split()** command to chop this string into two parts. The parts before and after the comma will become separate items that you can store in a list called **current_event**. Add this line after your code in Step 10.

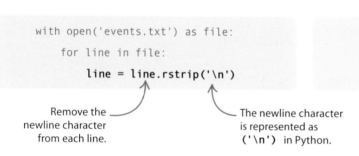

```
    for line in file:
        line = line.rstrip('\n')
        current_event = line.split(',')
```

Split each event into two parts at the comma.

Datetime module

Python's **datetime** module is very useful if you want to do calculations involving dates and time. For example, do you know what day of the week you were born on? Try typing this into the Python shell to find out.

Type your birthday in this format: year, month, day.

```
>>> from datetime import *
>>> print(date(2007, 12, 4).weekday())
1
```

This number represents the day of the week, where Monday is 0 and Sunday is 6. So 4 December 2007 was a Tuesday.

REMEMBER

List positions

When Python numbers the items in a list, it starts from 0. So the first item in your **current_event** list, "Halloween", is in position 0, while the second item, "31/10/2017", is in position 1. That's why the code turns **current_event[1]** into a date.

Sorry! You are not on the list.

12 **Using datetime**

The event Halloween is stored in **current_event** as a list containing two items: "Halloween" and "31/10/2017". Use the **datetime** module to convert the second item in the list (in position 1) from a string into a form that Python can understand as a date. Add these lines of code at the bottom of the function.

Turns the second item in the list from a string into a date.

```
current_event = line.split(',')
event_date = datetime.strptime(current_event[1], '%d/%m/%y').date()
current_event[1] = event_date
```

Set the second item in the list to be the date of the event.

13 **Add the event to the list**

Now the **current_event** list holds two things: the name of the event (as a string) and the date of the event. Add **current_event** to the list of events. Here's the whole code for the **get_events()** function.

```
def get_events():
    list_events = []
    with open('events.txt') as file:
        for line in file:
            line = line.rstrip('\n')
            current_event = line.split(',')
            event_date = datetime.strptime(current_event[1], '%d/%m/%y').date()
            current_event[1] = event_date
            list_events.append(current_event)
    return list_events
```

After this line is run, the program loops back to read the next line from the file.

After all the lines have been read, the function hands over the complete list of events to the program.

Setting the countdown

In the next stage of building Countdown Calendar you'll create a function to count the number of days between today and your important events. You'll also write the code to display the events on the **Tkinter** canvas.

20 days to Christmas!

The function is given two dates.

14 Count the days

Create a function to count the number of days between two dates. The **datetime** module makes this easy, as it can add dates together or subtract one from another. Type the code shown here below your **get_events()** function. It will store the number of days as a string in the variable **time_between**.

```python
def days_between_dates(date1, date2):
    time_between = str(date1 - date2)
```

This variable stores the result as a string.

The dates are subtracted to give the number of days between them.

15 Split the string

If Halloween is 27 days away, the string stored in **time_between** would look like this: **'27 days, 0:00:00'** (the zeros refer to hours, minutes, and seconds). Only the number at the beginning of the string is important, so you can use the **split()** command again to get to the part you need. Type the code highlighted below after the code in Step 14. It turns the string into a list of three items: **'27'**, **'days'**, **'0:00:00'**. The list is stored in **number_of_days**.

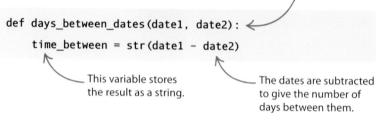

Oops! I've snipped the string!

```python
def days_between_dates(date1, date2):
    time_between = str(date1 - date2)
    number_of_days = time_between.split(' ')
```

This time the string is split at each blank space.

16 Return the number of days

To finish off this function, you just need to return the value stored in position 0 of the list. In the case of Halloween, that's 27. Add this line of code to the end of the function.

```python
def days_between_dates(date1, date2):
    time_between = str(date1 - date2)
    number_of_days = time_between.split(' ')
    return number_of_days[0]
```

The number of days between the dates is held at position 0 in the list.

17 Get the events

Now that you've written all the functions, you can use them to write the main part of the program. Put these two lines at the bottom of your file. The first line calls (runs) the **get_events()** function and stores the list of calendar events in a variable called **events**. The second line uses the **datetime** module to get today's date and stores it in a variable called **today**.

Use a backslash character if you need to split a long line of code over two lines.

Don't forget to save your work.

```
c.create_text(100, 50, anchor='w', fill='orange', \
font='Arial 28 bold underline', text='My Countdown Calendar')


events = get_events()
today = date.today()
```

Whoa! I've come first in class!

18 Display the results

Next calculate the number of days until each event and display the results on the screen. You need to do this for every event in the list, so use a **for** loop. For each event in the list, call the **days_between_dates()** function and store the result in a variable called **days_until**. Then use the **Tkinter create_text()** function to display the result on the screen. Add this code right after the code from Step 17.

The code runs for each event in the list called events.

Gets the name of the event.

Uses the **days_between_dates()** function to calculate the number of days between the event and today's date.

```
for event in events:
    event_name = event[0]
    days_until = days_between_dates(event[1], today)
    display = 'It is %s days until %s' % (days_until, event_name)
    c.create_text(100, 100, anchor='w', fill='lightblue', \
                  font='Arial 28 bold', text=display)
```

Creates a string to hold what we want to show on the screen.

This character makes the code go over two lines.

Displays the text on the screen at position (100, 100).

19 Test the program

Now try running the code. It looks like all the text lines are written on top of each other. Can you work out what's gone wrong? How could you solve it?

My Countdown Calendar

It is 98 days until Splash Test

20 Spread it out

The problem is that all the text is displayed at the same location (100, 100). If we create a variable called `vertical_space` and increase its value every time the program goes through the `for` loop, it will increase the value of the y coordinate and space out the text further down the screen. That'll solve it!

My Countdown Calendar

It is 26 days until Halloween
It is 57 days until Spanish Test
It is 138 days until School Trip
It is 98 days until My Birthday

```
vertical_space = 100

for event in events:
    event_name = event[0]
    days_until = days_between_dates(event[1], today)
    display = 'It is %s days until %s' % (days_until, event_name)
    c.create_text(100, vertical_space, anchor='w', fill='lightblue', \
                font='Arial 28 bold', text=display)

    vertical_space = vertical_space + 30
```

21 Start the countdown!

That's it – you've written all the code you need for Countdown Calendar. Now run your program and try it out.

Hacks and tweaks

Try these hacks and tweaks to make Countdown Calendar even more useful. Some of them are harder than others, so there are a few useful tips to help you out.

▷ **Repaint the canvas**

You can edit the background colour of your canvas and really jazz up the look of the program's display. Change the `c = Canvas` line of the code.

```
c = Canvas(root, width=800, height=800, bg='green')
```

You can change the background colour to any colour of your choice.

▷ Sort it!

You can tweak your code so that the events get sorted into the order they'll be happening. Add this line of code before the **for** loop. It uses the **sort()** function to organize the events in ascending order, from the smallest number of days remaining to the largest.

```
vertical_space = 100

events.sort(key=lambda x: x[1])

for event in events:
```

Sort the list in order of days to go and not by the name of the events.

▽ Restyle the text

Give your user interface a fresh new look by changing the size, colour, and style of the title text.

Pick your favourite colour.

```
c.create_text(100, 50, anchor='w', fill='pink', font='Courier 36 bold underline', \
              text='Sanjay\'s Diary Dates')
```

Change the title too if you like.

Try out a different font, such as Courier.

Guys, you're on in 10 minutes!

▽ Set reminders

It might be useful to highlight events that are happening really soon. Hack your code so that any events happening in the next week are shown in red.

```
for event in events:
    event_name = event[0]
    days_until = days_between_dates(event[1], today)
    display = 'It is %s days until %s' % (days_until, event_name)
    if (int(days_until) <= 7):
        text_col = 'red'
    else:
        text_col = 'lightblue'
    c.create_text(100, vertical_space, anchor='w', fill=text_col, \
                  font='Arial 28 bold', text=display)
```

The symbol <= means "is less than or equal to".

Display the text using the correct colour.

The **int()** function changes a string into a number. For example, it turns the string '5' into the number 5.

Ask the Expert

Can you name all the capital cities in the world? Or the players in your favourite sports team? Everyone's an expert on something. In this project, you'll code a program that can not only answer your questions, but also learn new things and become an expert.

You can ask me anything in the world.

What happens

An input box asks you to enter the name of a country. When you type in your answer, the program tells you what the capital city is. If the program doesn't know, it asks you to teach it the correct answer. The more people use the program, the smarter it gets!

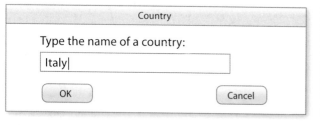

Country

Type the name of a country:

Italy|

OK   Cancel

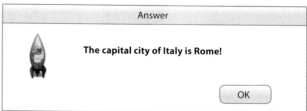

Answer

The capital city of Italy is Rome!

OK

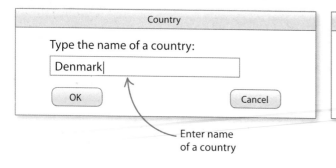

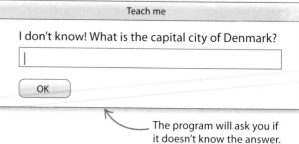

Country

Type the name of a country:

Denmark|

OK   Cancel

Enter name of a country

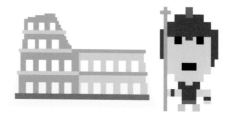

Teach me

I don't know! What is the capital city of Denmark?

|

OK

The program will ask you if it doesn't know the answer.

How it works

The program gets the information about capital cities from a text file. You'll use the **Tkinter** module to create the pop-up boxes that let the program and user communicate. When a new capital city is entered by a user, the information is added into the text file.

△ **Dictionaries**

You'll store the names of countries and their capitals in a dictionary. Dictionaries work a bit like lists, but each item in a dictionary has two parts, called a key and a value. It's usually quicker to look things up in a dictionary than it is to find something in a long list.

▷ **Communication**

The program uses two new **Tkinter** widgets. The first, **simpledialog()**, creates a pop-up box that asks the user to input the name of a country. The second, **messagebox()**, displays the capital city.

▽ **Ask the Expert flowchart**

When the program starts, it reads the data from a text file. It then uses an infinite loop to keep asking questions, and only stops when the user quits the program.

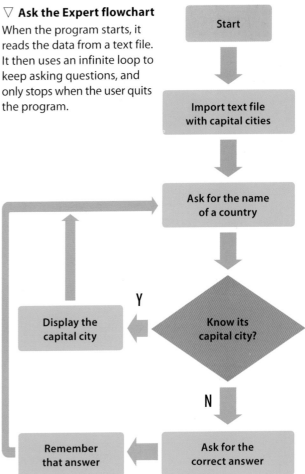

Start

Import text file with capital cities

Ask for the name of a country

Know its capital city?

Y — Display the capital city

N — Ask for the correct answer

Remember that answer

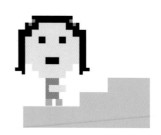

First steps

Follow these steps to build your own expert system using Python. You'll need to write a text file of country capitals, open a **Tkinter** window, and create a dictionary to store all the knowledge.

1 Prepare the text file

First make a text file to hold a list of capital cities of the world. Create a new file in IDLE and type in the following facts.

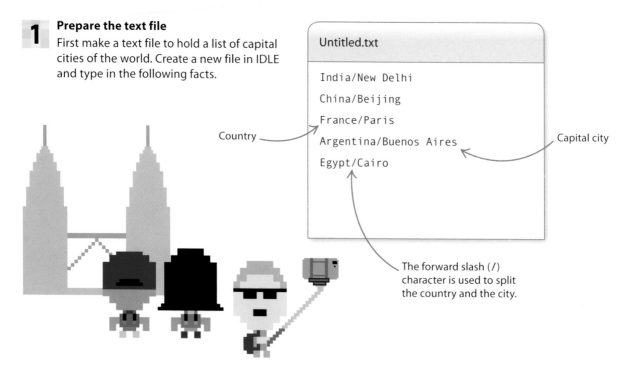

Untitled.txt

```
India/New Delhi
China/Beijing
France/Paris
Argentina/Buenos Aires
Egypt/Cairo
```

Country ⟵

Capital city ⟶

The forward slash (/) character is used to split the country and the city.

2 Save the text file

Save the file as "capital_data.txt". The program will get its specialist knowledge from this file.

Type "txt" at the end of the filename, instead of "py".

Save		
Save As:	capital_data.txt	▼
Tags:		
Where:		
	Cancel	Save

3 Create the Python file

To write the program, create a new file and save it as "ask_expert.py". Make sure you save it in the same folder as your text file.

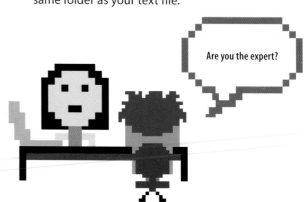

Are you the expert?

4 Import Tkinter **tools**

To make this program you'll need some widgets from the **Tkinter** module. Type this line at the top of your program.

Load these two widgets from the **Tkinter** module.

```
from tkinter import Tk, simpledialog, messagebox
```

5 Start Tkinter

Next add the following code to display the title of the project in the shell. **Tkinter** automatically creates an empty window. You don't need it for this project, so hide it with a clever line of code.

```
print('Ask the Expert - Capital Cities of the World')
root = Tk()
root.withdraw()
```

Hide the **Tkinter** window.

Create an empty **Tkinter** window.

Testing! Testing!

6 Test the code

Try running your code. You should see the name of the project displayed in the shell.

This creates an empty dictionary called **the_world**.

```
the_world = {}
```

Use curly brackets.

7 Set up a dictionary

Now type this line of code after the code you wrote for Step 5. The new code sets up the dictionary that will store the names of the countries and their capital cities.

I'll store all the information in here.

• • EXPERT TIPS

Using a dictionary

A dictionary is another way you can store information in Python. It is similar to a list, but each item has two parts: a key and a value. You can test it out by typing this into the shell window.

This is the key.

This is the value.

```
favourite_foods = {'Simon': 'pizza', 'Jill': 'pancakes', 'Roger': 'custard'}
```

A colon is used immediately after the key.

Each item in the dictionary is separated by a comma.

Dictionaries use curly brackets.

▽ **1.** To show the contents of a dictionary, you have to print it. Try printing **favourite_foods**.

```
print(favourite_foods)
```

Type this in the shell and hit return.

▽ **2.** Now add a new item to the dictionary: Julie and her favourite food. She likes biscuits.

```
favourite_foods['Julie'] = 'biscuits'
```

Key   Value

▽ **3.** Jill has changed her mind – her favourite food is now tacos. You can update this information in the dictionary.

```
favourite_foods['Jill'] = 'tacos'
```

Updated value

▽ **4.** Finally, you can look up Roger's favourite food in the dictionary by simply using his name as the key.

```
print(favourite_foods['Roger'])
```

Use the key to look up the value.

It's function time!

The next stage of the project involves creating the functions that you'll need to use in your program.

8 **File input**

You need a function to read in all the information stored in your text file. It will be similar to the one you used in Countdown Calendar to read in data from your events file. Add this code after the **Tkinter** import line.

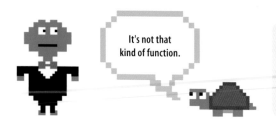

It's not that kind of function.

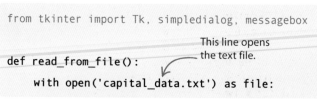

```
from tkinter import Tk, simpledialog, messagebox

def read_from_file():
    with open('capital_data.txt') as file:
```

This line opens the text file.

9. Line by line

Now use a **for** loop to go through the file line by line. Just as in Countdown Calendar, you must remove the invisible newline character. Then you need to store the values of country and city in two variables. Using the split command, the code will return the two values. You can store these values in two variables using one line of code.

```python
def read_from_file():
    with open('capital_data.txt') as file:
        for line in file:
            line = line.rstrip('\n')
            country, city = line.split('/')
```

This removes the newline character.

The "/" character splits the line.

This stores the word before "/" in the variable **country**.

This stores the word after "/" in the variable **city**.

10. Add data to the dictionary

At this stage, the variables **country** and **city** hold the information you need to add into the dictionary. For the first line in your text file, **country** would hold "India" and **city** would hold "New Delhi". Type this line of code to put them into the dictionary.

```python
def read_from_file():
    with open('capital_data.txt') as file:
        for line in file:
            line = line.rstrip('\n')
            country, city = line.split('/')
            the_world[country] = city
```

This is the value.

This is the key.

11. File output

When the user types in a capital city the program doesn't know about, you want the program to insert this new information into the text file. This is called file output. It works in a similar way to file input, but instead of reading the file, you write into it. Type this new function after the code you typed in Step 10.

```python
def write_to_file(country_name, city_name):
    with open('capital_data.txt', 'a') as file:
```

This function will add new country and capital city names to the text file.

The a means "append", or add, new information to the end of the file.

12 **Write to the file**

Now add a line of code to write the new information into the file. First the code will add a newline character, which tells the program to start a new line in the text file. Then it writes the name of the country followed by a forward slash (/) and the name of the capital city, such as Egypt/Cairo. Python automatically closes the text file once the information has been written into it.

Your files are safe with me!

```python
def write_to_file(country_name, city_name):
    with open('capital_data.txt', 'a') as file:
        file.write('\n' + country_name + '/' + city_name)
```

Code the main program

You've written all the functions you need, so it's time to start coding the main program.

Run the `read_from_file` function.

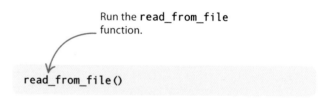

```python
read_from_file()
```

13 **Read the text file**

The first thing you want the program to do is to read the information from the text file. Add this line after the code you wrote in Step 7.

This is the box created by `simpledialog`.

14 **Start the infinite loop**

Next add the code below to create an infinite loop. Inside the loop is a function from the **Tkinter** module: `simpledialog.askstring()`. This function creates a box on the screen that displays information and gives a space for the user to type an answer. Test the code again. A box will appear asking you for the name of a country. It may be hidden behind the other windows.

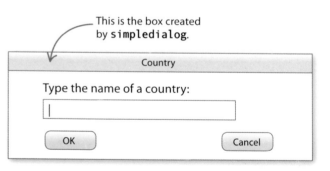

This appears in the box to tell the user what to do.

```python
read_from_file()


while True:
    query_country = simpledialog.askstring('Country', 'Type the name of a country:')
```

The answer the user types is stored in this variable.

This is the title of the box.

15 Know the answer?

Now add an **if** statement to see if the program knows the answer. This will check whether the country and its capital city are stored in the dictionary.

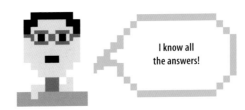

I know all the answers!

```
while True:
    query_country = simpledialog.askstring('Country', 'Type the name of a country:')


    if query_country in the_world:
```

Will return **True** if the country input by the user is stored in the the_world.

16 Display the correct answer

If the country is in **the_world**, you want the program to look up the correct answer and display it on the screen. To do this, use the **messagebox. showinfo()** function from the **Tkinter** module. This displays the message in a box with an OK button. Type this inside the **if** statement.

Using **query_country** as the key, this line looks up the answer from the dictionary.

Don't forget to save your work.

```
if query_country in the_world:
    result = the_world[query_country]
    messagebox.showinfo('Answer',
                'The capital city of ' + query_country + ' is ' + result + '!')
```

This is the title of the box.

This variable stores the answer (the value from the dictionary).

This message will be displayed inside the box.

17 Test it out

If your code has a bug, now would be a good time to catch it. When it asks you to name a country, type "France". Does it give you the correct answer? If it doesn't, look back over your code carefully and see if you can find out where it's gone wrong. What would happen if you typed in a country that wasn't in the text file? Try it out to see how the program responds.

It's a good time for a bug hunt!

18 Teach it

Finally, add a few more lines after the **if** statement. If the country isn't in the dictionary, the program asks the user to enter the name of its capital city. This capital city is added to the dictionary, so that the program remembers it for next time. Then the **write_to_file()** function adds the city to the text file.

Teach me the capital of Italy.

```python
    if query_country in the_world:
        result = the_world[query_country]
        messagebox.showinfo('Answer',
                            'The capital city of ' + query_country + ' is ' + result + '!')
    else:
        new_city = simpledialog.askstring('Teach me',
                                          'I don\'t know! ' +
                                          'What is the capital city of ' + query_country + '?')
        the_world[query_country] = new_city
        write_to_file(query_country, new_city)

root.mainloop()
```

Ask the user to type in the capital city and store it in **new_city**.

This adds **new_city** to the dictionary, using **query_country** as the key.

Write the new capital city into the text file, so that it gets added to the program's knowledge.

19 Run it

That's it. You've created a digital expert! Now run the code and start quizzing it!

Hacks and tweaks

Take your program to the next level and make it even smarter by trying out these suggestions.

I'm ready for my round-the-world tour!

▷ **Around the world**

Turn your program into a geographical genius by creating a text file that contains every country in the world and its capital city. Remember to put each entry on a new line in this format: country name/capital city.

▽ Capitalize

If the user forgets to use a capital letter to name the country, the program won't find the capital city. How can you solve this problem using code? Here's one way to do it.

```
query_country = simpledialog.askstring('Country', 'Type the name of a country:')
query_country = query_country.capitalize()
```

This function turns the first letter in a string into a capital letter.

```
sports_teams.txt

Castle United/Bobby Welsh
Dragon Rangers/Alex Andrews
Purple Giants/Sam Sloan
```

Coach's name

Team name

◁ Different data

At the moment, the program only knows about capital cities of the world. You can change that by editing the text file so that it stores facts about a subject you're an expert on. For example, you could teach it the names of famous sports teams and their coaches.

▷ Fact check

Your program currently adds new answers straight into the text file, but it can't check if the answers are correct. Tweak the code so that new answers are saved in a separate text file. Then you can check them later before adding them to the main text file. Here's how you can change the code.

```
def write_to_file(country_name, city_name):
    with open('new_data.txt', 'a') as file:
        file.write('\n' + country_name + '/' + city_name)
```

This stores the new answers in a different text file, called **new_data**.

They're right you know!

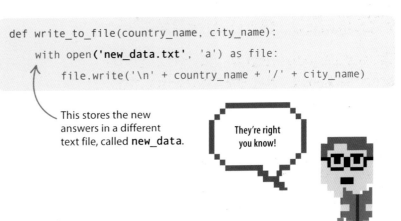

Secret Messages

Swap messages with your friends using the art of cryptography – changing the text of a message so that people who don't know your secret methods can't understand it!

What happens

The program will ask you if you want to create a secret message or reveal what a secret message says. It will then ask you to type in the message. If you choose to make a secret message, your message will be turned into what looks like total gibberish. But if you choose to reveal a message, nonsense will be turned into text you can read!

Cryptography

The word cryptography comes from the ancient Greek words for "hidden" and "writing". People have been using this technique to send secret messages for nearly 4,000 years. Here are some special terms used in cryptography:

Cipher – a set of instructions for altering a message to hide its meaning.
Encrypt – to hide the secret message.
Decrypt – to reveal the secret message.
Ciphertext – the message after it has been encrypted.
Plaintext – the message before it has been encrypted.

▷ **Share the code**
If you share your Python code with a friend, you'll be able to pass secret messages to each other.

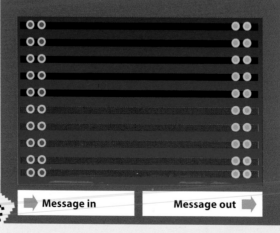

Message encrypter

Let's put this message in to scramble it.

➡ Message in   Message out ➡

I can't understand a word of this...

How it works

The program rearranges the order of letters in the message so that it can't be understood. It does this by working out which letters are in even or odd positions. Then it swaps the position of each pair of letters in the message, starting with the first two, then the next two, and so on. The program also makes encrypted messages readable again by switching the letters back to where they started.

I've mixed up all my letters.

In Python (which counts in a weird way, starting from 0), the first letter in the word is in an even position.

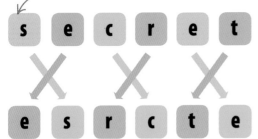

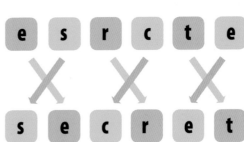

△ **Encryption**
When you run the code on your message, the program swaps each pair of letters, scrambling the meaning.

△ **Decryption**
When you or a friend decrypt the message, the program swaps the letters back to their original positions.

Message decrypter

➡ **Message in**   **Message out** ➡

I'll put this message through the decrypter to unscramble it!

It makes perfect sense now. What a brilliant machine!

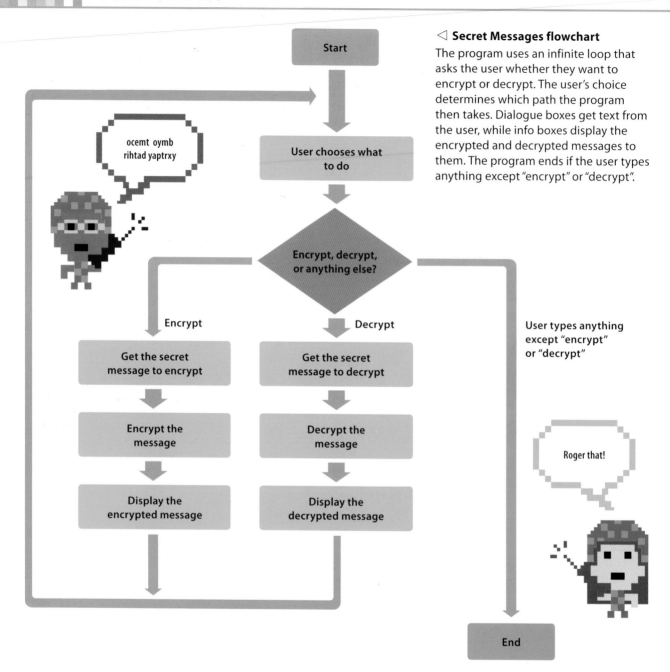

Start

User chooses what to do

ocemt oymb rihtad yaptrxy

Encrypt, decrypt, or anything else?

Encrypt

Get the secret message to encrypt

Encrypt the message

Display the encrypted message

Decrypt

Get the secret message to decrypt

Decrypt the message

Display the decrypted message

User types anything except "encrypt" or "decrypt"

Roger that!

End

◁ **Secret Messages flowchart**
The program uses an infinite loop that asks the user whether they want to encrypt or decrypt. The user's choice determines which path the program then takes. Dialogue boxes get text from the user, while info boxes display the encrypted and decrypted messages to them. The program ends if the user types anything except "encrypt" or "decrypt".

▷ **Mystery x**
The program needs the message to have an even number of characters. It checks the message and counts the characters. If there's an odd number of characters, it adds an x to the end to make it even. You and your fellow secret agents will know to ignore the x, so you won't be fooled!

Plaintext of the secret message is:

come to my party saturday afternoonx

OK

Making the GUI

You're going to write your code in two sections. First you'll set up some functions to get input from the user; then you'll write the code that does the encryption and decryption. Now let's get started – you never know when you might need to send a secret message to someone!

1 **Create a new file**
Open IDLE and create a new file. Save it as "secret_messages.py".

2 **Add the modules**
You need to import some widgets from Python's **Tkinter** module. This will let you use some of its GUI features, such as **messagebox** to display information to the user, and **simpledialog** to ask them questions. Type this line at the top of your file.

```python
from tkinter import messagebox, simpledialog, Tk
```

3 **Encrypt or decrypt?**
Now create a function, **get_task()**, to open a dialogue box that asks the user whether they want to encrypt or decrypt a message. Add the function under the code you added in Step 2.

This line asks the user to type in "encrypt" or "decrypt", then saves their response in the variable **task**.

```python
def get_task():
    task = simpledialog.askstring('Task', 'Do you want to encrypt or decrypt?')
    return task
```

Pass the value in **task** back to the code that used this function.

This word will appear as a title in the dialogue box.

4 **Get the message**
Create a new function, **get_message()**, to open a dialogue box asking the user to type in the message they want to encrypt or decrypt. Add this function under the code you added in Step 3.

This line asks the user to type the message, then saves it in the variable **message**.

```python
def get_message():
    message = simpledialog.askstring('Message', 'Enter the secret message: ')
    return message
```

Pass the value in **message** back to the code that used this function.

5   Start Tkinter
This command starts **Tkinter** and creates a **Tkinter** window. Type it below the function you made in Step 4.

```
root = Tk()
```

If you find the **Tkinter** window distracting, add the **root.withdraw** line you used in Ask the Expert.

6   Start the loop
Now that you've created your interface functions, add this infinite **while** loop to call (run) them in the correct order. Insert this code under the command you typed in Step 5.

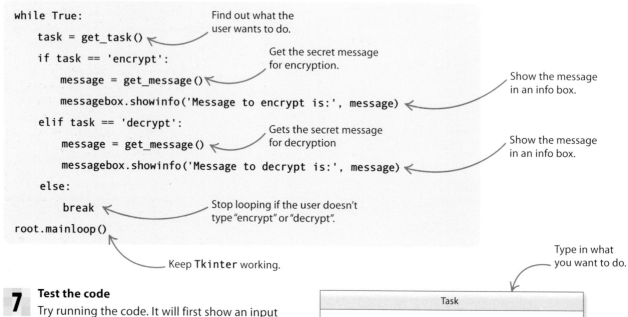

```
while True:
    task = get_task()
    if task == 'encrypt':
        message = get_message()
        messagebox.showinfo('Message to encrypt is:', message)
    elif task == 'decrypt':
        message = get_message()
        messagebox.showinfo('Message to decrypt is:', message)
    else:
        break
root.mainloop()
```

Find out what the user wants to do.

Get the secret message for encryption.

Show the message in an info box.

Gets the secret message for decryption

Show the message in an info box.

Stop looping if the user doesn't type "encrypt" or "decrypt".

Keep **Tkinter** working.

7   Test the code
Try running the code. It will first show an input box asking if you want to encrypt or decrypt. Then another input box will appear so that you can type in the secret message. Lastly, it will show the encrypted or decrypted message in an info box. If there's a problem, check your code carefully.

Type in what you want to do.

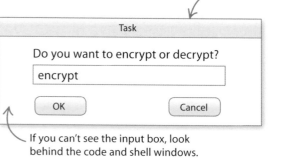

If you can't see the input box, look behind the code and shell windows.

Type the secret message.

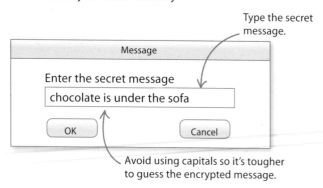

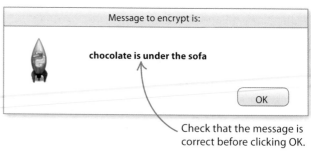

Avoid using capitals so it's tougher to guess the encrypted message.

Check that the message is correct before clicking OK.

Scramble the message!

Now that you've got your interface working, it's time to write the code that will encrypt and then decrypt your secret message.

Scrambled messages? I thought you said scrambled eggs!

8 **Is it even?**
You need to create a function to tell the program whether or not there's an even number of characters in your message. The function will use the modulo operator (**%**) to check if it can divide the number by 2 without leaving a remainder. If it can (True), then the number's even. Add this function under the code you typed in Step 2.

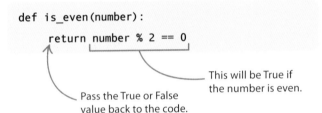

```
def is_even(number):
    return number % 2 == 0
```

Pass the True or False value back to the code.

This will be True if the number is even.

EXPERT TIPS
Modulo operator (%)

If you put the modulo operator (**%**) between two numbers, Python tells you the remainder when you divide the first number by the second. So 4 **%** 2 is 0, but 5 **%** 2 is 1, because there's 1 left over if you divide 5 by 2. Type these examples in the shell if you want to try them out.

9 **Get the even letters**
In this step, you'll make a function that takes a message and produces a list containing all the even-numbered letters. The function uses a **for** loop with a range that goes from 0 to **len(message)**, so that it checks all the letters in the string. Add this function under the code in Step 8.

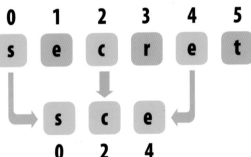

Make a list variable to store the even letters.

```
def get_even_letters(message):
    even_letters = []
    for counter in range(0, len(message)):
        if is_even(counter):
            even_letters.append(message[counter])
    return even_letters
```

Loop through every letter in the message.

If this is a letter in an even position, Python adds it to the end of the list of letters.

Pass the list of letters back to the code that called this function.

Don't forget to save your work.

10 Get the odd letters

Next you need to create a similar function to produce a list of all the odd-numbered letters in your message. Put this function under the code in Step 9.

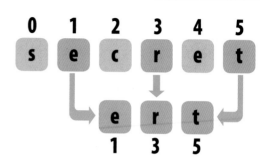

```python
def get_odd_letters(message):
    odd_letters = []
    for counter in range(0, len(message)):
        if not is_even(counter):
            odd_letters.append(message[counter])
    return odd_letters
```

11 Swap the letters round

Now that you've got even letters in one list and odd in another, you can use them to encrypt your message. The next function will take letters alternately from these lists and put them into a new list. But rather than assembling them in the original order, starting with an even letter, it'll start the message with an odd one. Type this function under the code in Step 10.

> **REMEMBER**
> ## Lists and length
> Python counts from 0 in lists and strings, and uses the function `len()` to find the length of a string. For example, if you type `len('secret')`, Python will tell you that the string `'secret'` is six characters long. But because the first letter is in position 0, the last letter is in position 5, not 6.

```python
def swap_letters(message):
    letter_list = []
    if not is_even(len(message)):
        message = message + 'x'
    even_letters = get_even_letters(message)
    odd_letters = get_odd_letters(message)
    for counter in range(0, int(len(message)/2)):
        letter_list.append(odd_letters[counter])
        letter_list.append(even_letters[counter])
    new_message = ''.join(letter_list)
    return new_message
```

Add an extra x to any message with an odd number of letters.

Loop through the lists of odd and even letters.

Add the next odd letter to the final message.

Add the next even letter to the final message.

The `join()` function turns the list of letters into a string.

▷ **How it works**
The `swap_letters()` function puts all the odd and even numbers into a new list, adding them alternately. It starts the list with the second letter in the word, which Python counts as an odd number.

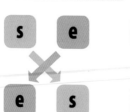

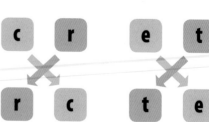

EXPERT TIPS

Integer positions

You use the value `len(message)/2` in your loop range because the even and odd letter lists are both half the length of the original message. You made sure the length of your message will always be even by getting the program to add an x when necessary, so it can be divided by 2. However, the result will be a float value (with a decimal point, such as 3.0 or 4.0) rather than an integer (a whole number, such as 3 or 4). Python gives an error if you try to use a float for the position of an item in a list, so use the `int()` function to convert it to an integer.

```
>>> mystring = 'secret'
>>> mystring[3.0]
Traceback (most recent call last):
  File "<pyshell#1>", line 1, in <module>
    mystring[3.0]
TypeError: string indices must be integers
```

This is the error message Python will give you if you use a float, such as 3.0, instead of an integer, such as 3.

12 **Update the loop**
The `swap_letters()` function has a really useful feature: if you run it on an encrypted message, it will decrypt it. So you can use this function to encrypt or decrypt messages depending on what the user wants to do. Make the following changes to the `while` loop you created in Step 6.

```
while True:
    task = get_task()
    if task == 'encrypt':
        message = get_message()
        encrypted = swap_letters(message)
        messagebox.showinfo('Ciphertext of the secret message is:', encrypted)
    elif task == 'decrypt':
        message = get_message()
        decrypted = swap_letters(message)
        messagebox.showinfo('Plaintext of the secret message is:', decrypted)
    else:
        break
root.mainloop()
```

Use `swap_letters()` to encrypt the message.

Display the encrypted message.

Uses `swap_letters()` to decrypt the message.

Display the decrypted message.

13 Run encryption

Test your program. Choose "encrypt" in the task window. When the message window pops up, enter the sort of message a spy might want to keep secret. Try: "meet me at the swings in the park at noon"!

14 Run decryption

If you select the encrypted text and copy it, you can choose the "decrypt" option next time round the loop. In the message window, paste the encrypted message and click OK. You'll then see the original message again.

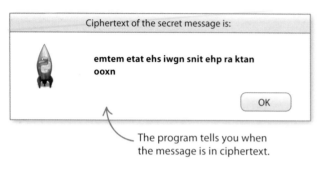

Ciphertext of the secret message is:

emtem etat ehs iwgn snit ehp ra ktan ooxn

OK

The program tells you when the message is in ciphertext.

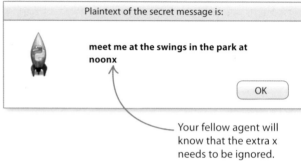

Plaintext of the secret message is:

meet me at the swings in the park at noonx

OK

Your fellow agent will know that the extra x needs to be ignored.

15 Decrypt this!

Your cipher program should now be working. To make sure, try decrypting the text shown here. You can now share your Python code with a friend and start sending secret messages!

ewlld no eoy uahevd ceyrtpdet ih sesrctem seaseg

oy uac nsu eelom nujci erom li ksai vnsibieli kn

Hacks and tweaks

Here are some ideas to make your secret messages even more difficult to read if they're intercepted by an enemy agent – such as a nosy brother or sister!

Let's remove the spaces and punctuation.

▷ **Remove the spaces**

One way to make your cipher more secure is to remove the spaces and any punctuation characters, such as full stops and commas. To do this, type your message without spaces and punctuation. Just make sure the friend you're swapping messages with knows that this is the plan.

! Helloworld

Reverse after swapping

To make it harder still for people to break your encryption, reverse the message after encrypting it with **swap_letters()**. To do this, you'll need to create two different functions – one to encrypt and one to decrypt.

Reverses the message once its letters have been swapped.

1 Encrypt function

The **encrypt()** function swaps the letters and then reverses the string. Type these lines under the **swap_letters()** function.

```
def encrypt(message):
    swapped_message = swap_letters(message)
    encrypted_message = ''.join(reversed(swapped_message))
    return encrypted_message
```

Undo the reverse action of the encrypt function by reversing the message again.

2 Decrypt function

Add this **decrypt()** function beneath the **encrypt()** function. It starts by reversing the encrypted message, and then uses **swap_letters()** to put the letters back in the right order.

```
def decrypt(message):
    unreversed_message = ''.join(reversed(message))
    decrypted_message = swap_letters(unreversed_message)
    return decrypted_message
```

This line puts the letters back in the right order.

3 Use the new functions

Now you need to update the infinite loop section of your program to use these functions instead of the **swap_letters()** function.

Don't forget to save your work.

```
while True:
    task = get_task()
    if task == 'encrypt':
        message = get_message()
        encrypted = encrypt(message)
        messagebox.showinfo('Ciphertext of the secret message is:', encrypted)
    elif task == 'decrypt':
        message = get_message()
        decrypted = decrypt(message)
    messagebox.showinfo('Plaintext of the secret message is:', decrypted)
    else:
        break
```

The new **encrypt()** function replaces **swap_letters()**.

The new **decrypt()** function replaces swap_letters().

Add "fake" letters

Another way to encrypt messages is to insert random letters between each pair of letters. So the word "secret" might become "stegciraelta" or "shevcarieste". Just as in the "Reverse after swapping" hack, you'll need two different functions – one to encrypt and one to decrypt.

shevcarieste!

s	e	c	r	e	t

s	t	e	g	c	i	r	a	e	l	t	a

All the green letters are fake ones.

1 Add another module

Import the **choice()** function from the random module. This will let you choose the fake letters from a list of letters. Type this line near the top of your file, under the command to import the Tkinter functions.

```
from tkinter import messagebox, simpledialog, Tk
from random import choice
```

2 Encrypt

To encrypt the message, you need to set up a list of fake letters to insert between the real ones. The code shown below will loop through the message, adding one real letter and one fake letter to the **encrypted_list** each time round.

Is this a fake letter?

```
def encrypt(message):
    encrypted_list = []
    fake_letters = ['a', 'b', 'c', 'd', 'e', 'f', 'g', 'i', 'r', 's', 't', 'u', 'v']
    for counter in range(0, len(message)):
        encrypted_list.append(message[counter])
        encrypted_list.append(choice(fake_letters))
    new_message = ''.join(encrypted_list)
    return new_message
```

Add fake letters between real letters.

Add a letter from the message to **encrypted_list**.

Add a fake letter to the **encrypted_list**.

Join the letters in **encrypted_list** into a string.

3 **Decrypt**

Decrypting the message is quite easy. In the encrypted version of your message, all the letters in even positions are letters from the original message. So you can use the **get_even_letters()** function to get them.

Decrypting letters is easy.

```
def decrypt(message):
    even_letters = get_even_letters(message)
    new_message = ''.join(even_letters)
    return new_message
```

Get the original message's letters.

Join the letters in **even_letters** into a string.

4 **Use the new functions**

Now you need to update the infinite loop section of your program to use the new **encrypt()** and **decrypt()** functions, instead of **swap_letters()**. To do this, make these changes to your code.

I must update my infinite loop!

```
while True:
    task = get_task()
    if task == 'encrypt':
        message = get_message()
        encrypted = encrypt(message)
        messagebox.showinfo('Ciphertext of the secret message is:', encrypted)
    elif task == 'decrypt':
        message = get_message()
        decrypted = decrypt(message)
        messagebox.showinfo('Plaintext of the secret message is:', decrypted)
    else:
        break
root.mainloop()
```

The new **encrypt()** function replaces **swap_letters()**.

The new **decrypt()** function replaces **swap_letters()**.

▷ **Multi-encryption**

To make things even more complex, you can modify your code so that it combines all the different hacks and tweaks from this section. For example, it could add fake letters, swap the letters, and then reverse them!

My secret codes are safer now!

Screen Pet

Have you ever wished you had a pet to keep you company while doing your homework on your computer? In this project, you'll create a pet that "lives" in a corner of your computer screen. It will keep you busy, because you'll need to look after your pet to keep it happy.

△ **Happy face**
If you "stroke it" with the mouse-pointer, Screen Pet beams and blushes.

What happens

When you start the program, Screen Pet will sit there, with a little smile on its face, blinking at you. Your cute, sky-blue companion will change its expression from normal (below) to happy, cheeky, or sad, depending on how you interact with it on the screen. But don't worry, it's friendly – it won't bite if it gets bored!

△ **Cheeky face**
If you double-click on it to "tickle" it, the cheeky pet sticks out its tongue.

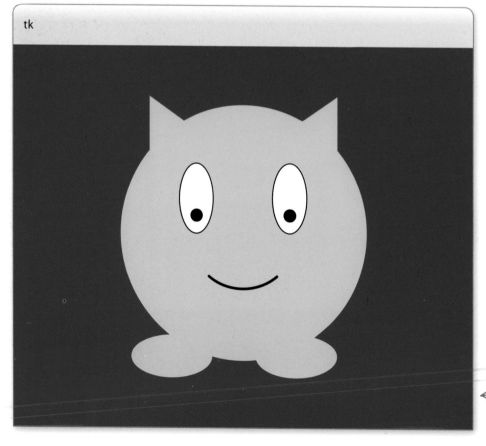

tk

△ **Sad face**
If you ignore it, Screen Pet will become sad. Stroking it will cheer it up again.

Screen Pet appears in a Tkinter window.

How it works

Running `Tkinter`'s `root.mainloop()` function sets up a `while` loop that keeps checking for input from the user. The loop keeps going until you close the main `Tkinter` window. This is also how you were able to make a GUI (graphical user interface) that reacted to a user clicking on a button or entering text in Ask the Expert.

▷ **Mainloop animation**
You can also animate images in a `Tkinter` window using the `root.mainloop()` function. By telling it to run functions that change the image at set times, you can make Screen Pet appear to move by itself.

LINGO

Event-driven program

Screen Pet is an event-driven program, which means that the things it does and the order it does them in depend on input from the user. The program looks for inputs, such as keypresses and mouse-clicks, then calls a different function to handle each one. Word-processing programs, video games, and drawing programs are all examples of event-driven programs.

▽ **Screen Pet flowchart**
The flowchart shows the sequence of actions and decisions, and how user inputs affect them. The program runs in an endless loop. It uses an ever-changing happiness variable to keep track of the pet's mood.

Get a move on!

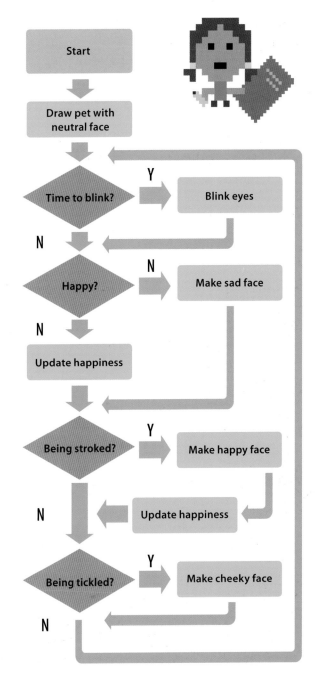

Start

Draw pet with neutral face

Time to blink? — **Y** → Blink eyes

N

Happy? — **N** → Make sad face

N

Update happiness

Being stroked? — **Y** → Make happy face

N

Update happiness

Being tickled? — **Y** → Make cheeky face

N

Draw your Screen Pet

Let's get started. First you need to create the window where your Screen Pet will live. Then you'll write some code to draw the pet on the screen.

Keep still while I paint you!

1 **Create a new file**
Open IDLE. Go to the File menu and select New File, then save the file as "screen_pet.py".

This line imports the parts of the **Tkinter** module that you'll need in this project.

2 **Add the Tkinter module**
You need to import parts of Python's **Tkinter** module at the start of your program. Type this code to bring in **Tkinter** and open a window where your Screen Pet will live.

```
from tkinter import HIDDEN, NORMAL, Tk, Canvas
root = Tk()
```

This line starts **Tkinter** and opens a window.

The canvas will be 400 pixels wide and 400 pixels high.

The background colour will be dark blue.

3 **Make a new canvas**
In the window, make a dark blue canvas called "c", on which you'll draw your pet. Add this code after the line that opens the **Tkinter** window. These four lines of new code are the start of the main part of your program.

```
from tkinter import HIDDEN, NORMAL, Tk, Canvas
root = Tk()
c = Canvas(root, width=400, height=400)
c.configure(bg='dark blue', highlightthickness=0)
c.pack()
root.mainloop()
```

This command arranges things within the **Tkinter** window.

Any commands that start with **c.** relate to the canvas.

4 **Run it**
Now try running the program. What do you notice? The code should just show a plain, dark-blue window. It looks a bit dull and empty at the moment – what you need is a pet!

This line starts the function that looks out for input events, such as mouse-clicks.

tk

Don't forget to save your work.

5 **Get drawing**
To draw your pet, add these instructions above the last two lines of code. There's a separate command for each body part. The numbers, called coordinates, tell `Tkinter` what to draw and where to draw it.

Storing the body colour in the variable **c.body_color** means you don't have to keep typing in `'SkyBlue1'`.

```
c.configure(bg='dark blue', highlightthickness=0)
c.body_color = 'SkyBlue1'
body = c.create_oval(35, 20, 365, 350, outline=c.body_color, fill=c.body_color)
ear_left = c.create_polygon(75, 80, 75, 10, 165, 70, outline=c.body_color, fill=c.body_color)
ear_right = c.create_polygon(255, 45, 325, 10, 320, 70, outline=c.body_color, \
                        fill=c.body_color)
foot_left = c.create_oval(65, 320, 145, 360, outline=c.body_color, fill= c.body_color)
foot_right = c.create_oval(250, 320, 330, 360, outline=c.body_color, fill= c.body_color)

eye_left = c.create_oval(130, 110, 160, 170, outline='black', fill='white')
pupil_left = c.create_oval(140, 145, 150, 155, outline='black', fill='black')
eye_right = c.create_oval(230, 110, 260, 170, outline='black', fill='white')
pupil_right = c.create_oval(240, 145, 250, 155, outline='black', fill='black')

mouth_normal = c.create_line(170, 250, 200, 272, 230, 250, smooth=1, width=2, state=NORMAL)
c.pack()
```

In the code, "left" and "right" refer to the left and right of the window as you look at it.

These pairs of coordinates define the start, mid-point, and end of the mouth.

The mouth is a smooth line, 2 pixels wide.

Tkinter coordinates

The drawing instructions use x and y coordinates. In `Tkinter`, the x coordinates start at 0 on the left and increase as you move across the window, until they reach 400 on the far right. The y coordinates start at 0 at the top. They get bigger as you move down, until they reach 400 at the bottom.

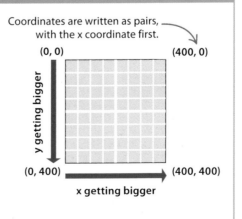

Coordinates are written as pairs, with the x coordinate first.

(0, 0)   (400, 0)

y getting bigger

(0, 400)   (400, 400)

x getting bigger

tk

6 **Run it again**
Run the program again and you should see Screen Pet sitting in the middle of the `Tkinter` window.

Blinking pet

Your Screen Pet looks cute, but it's not doing anything!
Let's write some code to get it blinking. You'll need to
create two functions: one to open and shut the eyes, the
other to tell them how long to stay open and shut for.

tk

7 **Open and close the eyes**
Create this function, `toggle_eyes()`, at the top of your file,
under the first line of code. It makes the eyes look closed by
hiding the pupils and filling the eyes with the same colour as the
body. It also switches the eyes between being open and closed.

To blink, the eyes fill
with sky blue and the
pupils disappear

First the code checks the
eyes' current colour: white is
open, blue is closed.

This line sets the eyes'
new_color to the
opposite value.

Now the code
checks if the current
state of the pupils is
NORMAL (visible) or
HIDDEN (not visible).

```
from tkinter import HIDDEN, NORMAL, Tk, Canvas


def toggle_eyes():
    current_color = c.itemcget(eye_left, 'fill')
    new_color = c.body_color if current_color == 'white' else 'white'
    current_state = c.itemcget(pupil_left, 'state')
    new_state = NORMAL if current_state == HIDDEN else HIDDEN
    c.itemconfigure(pupil_left, state=new_state)
    c.itemconfigure(pupil_right, state=new_state)
    c.itemconfigure(eye_left, fill=new_color)
    c.itemconfigure(eye_right, fill=new_color)
```

These lines change the
visibility of the pupils.

This line sets the
pupils' **new_
state** to the
opposite value.

These lines change the
eyes' fill colour.

Toggle light on!

Just you toggle that
light back off!

8 **Realistic blinking**

The eyes need to close only briefly and stay open for a while between blinks. Add this function, **blink()**, under the code you typed in Step 7. It blinks the eyes for a quarter of a second (250 milliseconds), then finishes with a command that tells **mainloop()** to call it again after 3 seconds (3,000 milliseconds).

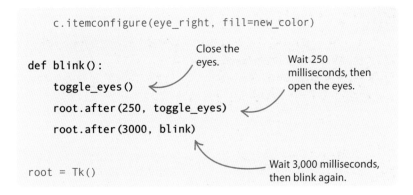

```
c.itemconfigure(eye_right, fill=new_color)
```

Close the eyes.

Wait 250 milliseconds, then open the eyes.

```
def blink():
    toggle_eyes()
    root.after(250, toggle_eyes)
    root.after(3000, blink)

root = Tk()
```

Wait 3,000 milliseconds, then blink again.

9 **Animate!**

Put this line in the main part of your program, just above the last line. Now run the program. Your pet will come to life after 1 second (1,000 milliseconds) and sit there blinking until you close the window.

```
root.after(1000, blink)
root.mainloop()
```

Wait 1,000 milliseconds, then start blinking.

Changing moods

Screen Pet looks quite happy just now, with its little smile, but let's cheer it up even more. We'll give it a bigger, beaming smile and bright, rosy cheeks.

10 **Make a happy face**

Add this code to the part of the program that draws Screen Pet, after the line that creates the "normal" mouth. As well as a happy mouth and pink cheeks, it also draws a sad mouth. They will all remain hidden for now.

Create a happy mouth.　　　　Create a sad mouth.

```
mouth_normal = c.create_line(170, 250, 200, 272, 230, 250, smooth=1, width=2, state=NORMAL)
mouth_happy = c.create_line(170, 250, 200, 282, 230, 250, smooth=1, width=2, state=HIDDEN)
mouth_sad = c.create_line(170, 250, 200, 232, 230, 250, smooth=1, width=2, state=HIDDEN)

cheek_left = c.create_oval(70, 180, 120, 230, outline='pink', fill='pink', state=HIDDEN)
cheek_right = c.create_oval(280, 180, 330, 230, outline='pink', fill='pink', state=HIDDEN)
```

These lines create pink, blushing cheeks.

```
c.pack()
```

11 Show the happy face

Next, create a function called **show_happy ()** to reveal the happy expression when you move the mouse-pointer over Screen Pet as if you were stroking it. Type this code beneath the **blink ()** function you added in Step 8.

Event handler

The function **show_happy ()** is an event handler. This means it's only called when a particular event happens, so that it can deal with it. In your code, stroking your pet calls **show_happy ()**. In real life, you might call a "mop the floor" function to handle a "spill drink" event!

> I hate mopping up!

The **if** line checks to see if the mouse-pointer is over the pet.

event.x and **event.y** are the coordinates of the mouse-pointer.

```
root.after(3000, blink)


def show_happy(event):
    if (20 <= event.x <= 350) and (20 <= event.y <= 350):
        c.itemconfigure(cheek_left, state=NORMAL)
        c.itemconfigure(cheek_right, state=NORMAL)
        c.itemconfigure(mouth_happy, state=NORMAL)
        c.itemconfigure(mouth_normal, state=HIDDEN)
        c.itemconfigure(mouth_sad, state=HIDDEN)
    return
```

Show the pink cheeks.

Show the happy mouth.

Hide the normal mouth.

Hide the sad mouth.

Focus

Tkinter won't be able to spot you moving the mouse-pointer over the window to stroke Screen Pet unless the window is "in focus". You can get it in focus by clicking once anywhere in the window.

> The window is in focus!

12 Happy moves

When the program starts, Screen Pet blinks without you doing anything. But to get it to look happy when it's being stroked, you need to tell it what event to look out for. **Tkinter** calls the mouse-pointer moving over its window a **<Motion>** event. You need to link this to the handler function by using **Tkinter**'s **bind ()** command. Add this line to the main part of your program. Then run the code and stroke the pet to try it out.

```
c.pack()


c.bind('<Motion>', show_happy)


root.after(1000, blink)

root.mainloop()
```

This command links the moving mouse-pointer to the happy face.

Hide the happy face

You only want Screen Pet to look really happy when you're actually stroking it. Add a new function, **hide_happy ()**, below the code for **show_happy ()**. This new code will set Screen Pet's expression back to normal.

Don't forget to save your work.

```
def hide_happy(event):
    c.itemconfigure(cheek_left, state=HIDDEN)
    c.itemconfigure(cheek_right, state=HIDDEN)
    c.itemconfigure(mouth_happy, state=HIDDEN)
    c.itemconfigure(mouth_normal, state=NORMAL)
    c.itemconfigure(mouth_sad, state=HIDDEN)
    return
```

Hide the pink cheeks.

Hide the happy mouth.

Show the normal mouth.

Hide the sad mouth.

Call the function

Type this line to call **hide_happy ()** when the mouse-pointer leaves the window. It links **Tkinter**'s **<Leave>** event to **hide_happy ()**. Now test your code.

```
c.bind('<Motion>', show_happy)
c.bind('<Leave>', hide_happy)


root.after(1000, blink)
```

What a cheek!

So far, your pet has been very well behaved. Let's give it a cheeky personality! You can add some code that will make Screen Pet stick its tongue out and cross its eyes when you tickle it by double-clicking on it.

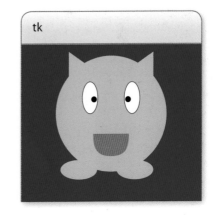

Draw the tongue

Add these lines to the code that draws Screen Pet, under the line that creates the sad mouth. The program will draw the tongue in two parts, a rectangle and an oval.

```
mouth_sad = c.create_line(170, 250, 200, 232, 230, 250, smooth=1, width=2, state=HIDDEN)
tongue_main = c.create_rectangle(170, 250, 230, 290, outline='red', fill='red', state=HIDDEN)
tongue_tip = c.create_oval(170, 285, 230, 300, outline='red', fill='red', state=HIDDEN)


cheek_left = c.create_oval(70, 180, 120, 230, outline='pink', fill='pink', state=HIDDEN)
```

16 Set up flags

Add two flag variables to the code to keep track of whether Screen Pet's eyes are crossed or its tongue is out. Type them just above the line that tells Screen Pet to start blinking, which you added to the main part of the code in Step 9.

```
c.eyes_crossed = False
c.tongue_out = False


root.after(1000, blink)
```

These are the flag variables for the pupils and the tongue.

17 Toggle the tongue

This function toggles Screen Pet's tongue between being out and in. Put the code shown below above the **show_happy ()** function that you created in Step 11.

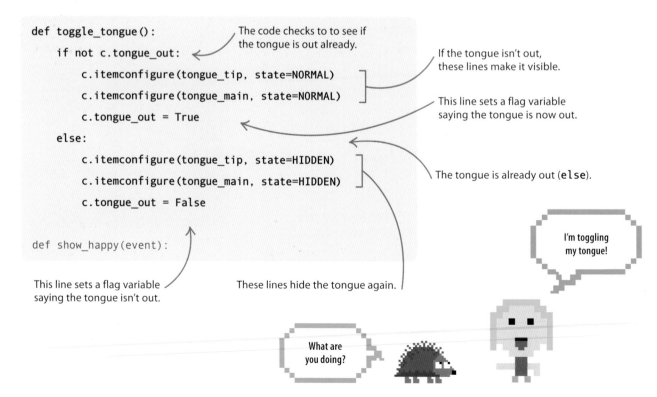

```
def toggle_tongue ():
    if not c.tongue_out:
        c.itemconfigure(tongue_tip, state=NORMAL)
        c.itemconfigure(tongue_main, state=NORMAL)
        c.tongue_out = True
    else:
        c.itemconfigure(tongue_tip, state=HIDDEN)
        c.itemconfigure(tongue_main, state=HIDDEN)
        c.tongue_out = False

def show_happy (event):
```

The code checks to to see if the tongue is out already.

If the tongue isn't out, these lines make it visible.

This line sets a flag variable saying the tongue is now out.

The tongue is already out (**else**).

This line sets a flag variable saying the tongue isn't out.

These lines hide the tongue again.

I'm toggling my tongue!

What are you doing?

```
root.after(3000, blink)
```

The code checks to see if the eyes are crossed already.

```
def toggle_pupils():
    if not c.eyes_crossed:
        c.move(pupil_left, 10, -5)
        c.move(pupil_right, -10, -5)
        c.eyes_crossed = True
    else:
        c.move(pupil_left, -10, 5)
        c.move(pupil_right, 10, 5)
        c.eyes_crossed = False
```

If the pupils aren't crossed, this line moves them in.

These lines move the pupils back to normal.

This line sets a flag variable saying the eyes are crossed.

The eyes are already crossed (**else**).

This line sets a flag saying the eyes aren't crossed.

18 **Toggle the pupils**
For the cross-eyed look, the pupils need to point inwards. This **toggle_pupils()** function will switch Screen Pet's pupils between pointing inwards and looking normal. Type it below the **blink()** function you added in Step 8.

Don't forget to save your work.

19 **Coordinate the cheekiness**
Now create a function to get Screen Pet to stick its tongue out and cross its eyes at the same time. Type this code under the **toggle_tongue()** function you added in Step 17. Use the **root.after()** function to make Screen Pet go back to normal after 1 second (1,000 milliseconds), like you did in **blink()**.

```
def cheeky(event):
    toggle_tongue()
    toggle_pupils()
    hide_happy(event)
    root.after(1000, toggle_tongue)
    root.after(1000, toggle_pupils)
    return
```

Stick the tongue out.

Cross the pupils.

Hide the happy face.

Put the tongue back in after 1,000 milliseconds.

Uncross the pupils after 1,000 milliseconds.

20 **Link double-clicks to cheekiness**
To trigger Screen Pet's cheeky expression, link any double-click event to the **cheeky()** function. Put this new line just below the line you added in Step 14 to hide Screen Pet's happy face. Run the code and double-click to see the cheekiness!

```
c.bind('<Motion>', show_happy)
c.bind('<Leave>', hide_happy)
c.bind('<Double-1>', cheeky)
```

<Double-1> is **Tkinter**'s name for a double-click in the window with the mouse.

Sad pet

Finally make Screen Pet notice if you don't pay any attention to it. After nearly a minute without being stroked, your poor, neglected pet will show its sad face!

tk

21

Set up a happiness level

Put this line of code just above the flag variables you added to the main part of the program in Step 16. It creates a happiness level for Screen Pet and sets the level at 10 when you run the program and draw the pet.

```
c.happy_level = 10
c.eyes_crossed = False
```

Screen Pet starts with a happiness level of 10.

22

Create a new command

Type this line below the command you added in Step 9 that starts Screen Pet blinking. It tells `mainloop()` to call the function `sad()`, which you'll add in Step 23, after 5 seconds (5,000 milliseconds).

```
root.after(1000, blink)
root.after(5000, sad)
root.mainloop()
```

Look at that poor, sad, neglected pet!

23

Write a sad function

Add this function, `sad()`, beneath `hide_happy()`. It checks to see if `c.happy_level` is 0 yet. If it is, it changes Screen Pet's expression to a sad one. If it's not, it subtracts 1 from `c.happy_level`. Like `blink()`, it reminds `mainloop()` to call it again after 5 seconds.

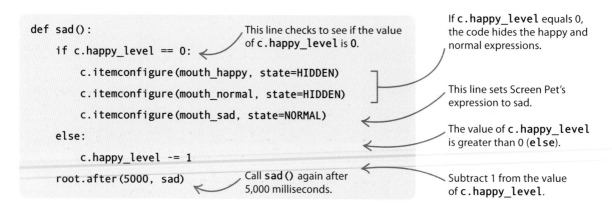

```
def sad():
    if c.happy_level == 0:
        c.itemconfigure(mouth_happy, state=HIDDEN)
        c.itemconfigure(mouth_normal, state=HIDDEN)
        c.itemconfigure(mouth_sad, state=NORMAL)
    else:
        c.happy_level -= 1
    root.after(5000, sad)
```

This line checks to see if the value of `c.happy_level` is 0.

If `c.happy_level` equals 0, the code hides the happy and normal expressions.

This line sets Screen Pet's expression to sad.

The value of `c.happy_level` is greater than 0 (`else`).

Subtract 1 from the value of `c.happy_level`.

Call `sad()` again after 5,000 milliseconds.

Cheer up, Screen Pet!
Is there any way to stop Screen Pet from getting sad? Or cheer it up when it's miserable? Luckily there is – you just click into its window and stroke it. Add this line of code to the **show_happy ()** function you wrote in Step 11. Now the function will reset the value of the variable **c.happy_level** back to 10 and make Screen Pet show its happy face again. Run the code to see your pet get sad, then cheer it up by stroking it.

Don't forget to save
your work.

```
c.itemconfigure(mouth_normal, state = HIDDEN)
c.itemconfigure(mouth_sad, state = HIDDEN)
c.happy_level = 10

return
```

This line puts the happiness
level back up to 10.

Hacks and tweaks

Is Screen Pet your ideal pet now? If not, you can change the way it behaves or add some extra features! Here are a few ideas for personalizing your Screen Pet.

Be friendly, not cheeky

Maybe you'd rather not have a cheeky pet? Get Screen Pet to give you a friendly wink instead of making a rude face when you double-click on it.

1 Add this function underneath the **blink ()** function. It's similar to the **blink ()** code, but it will only toggle one eye.

```
def toggle_left_eye():
    current_color = c.itemcget(eye_left, 'fill')
    new_color = c.body_color if current_color == 'white'   else 'white'
    current_state = c.itemcget(pupil_left, 'state')
    new_state = NORMAL if current_state == HIDDEN else HIDDEN
    c.itemconfigure(pupil_left, state=new_state)
    c.itemconfigure(eye_left, fill=new_color)
```

2 The next function closes and opens the left eye once to make Screen Pet wink. Type it below **toggle_left_eye()**.

```
def wink(event):
    toggle_left_eye()
    root.after(250, toggle_left_eye)
```

3 Remember to change the command that binds the double-click event (**<Double-1>**) to **wink()** instead of **cheeky()** in the main part of the program.

```
c.bind('<Double-1>', wink)
```

Change **cheeky** to **wink** here.

Rainbow pets

It's easy to make Screen Pet a different colour by changing the value of **c.body_color**. If you can't decide what colour to choose, you can add a function that keeps changing Screen Pet's colour nonstop!

1 First add a line to import Python's **random** module. Put it under the line that loads the project's **Tkinter** features.

```
from tkinter import HIDDEN, NORMAL, Tk, Canvas
import random
```

2 Now type a new function, **change_color()**, just above the main part of the code. It picks a new value for **c.body_color** from the list **pet_colors**. Then it redraws Screen Pet's body using the new colour. Because it uses **random.choice**, you can never be sure what colour the pet will be next!

List of possible colours for Screen Pet

This line chooses another colour from the list at random.

```
def change_color():
    pet_colors = ['SkyBlue1', 'tomato', 'yellow', 'purple', 'green', 'orange']
    c.body_color = random.choice(pet_colors)]
    c.itemconfigure(body, outline=c.body_color, fill=c.body_color)
    c.itemconfigure(ear_left, outline=c.body_color, fill=c.body_color)
    c.itemconfigure(ear_right, outline=c.body_color, fill=c.body_color)
    c.itemconfigure(foot_left, outline=c.body_color, fill=c.body_color)
    c.itemconfigure(foot_right, outline=c.body_color, fill=c.body_color)
    root.after(5000, change_color)
```

These lines set Screen Pet's body, feet, and ears to the new colour.

The program calls **change_color()** again after 5,000 milliseconds (5 seconds).

3 Finally add this just above the last line in the main part of the program to get `mainloop()` to call `change_color()` 5 seconds (5,000 milliseconds) after the program starts.

```
root.after(5000, change_color)
```

Your pet will begin changing colour 5 seconds after the program starts.

4 You might want to alter the values in the code so that Screen Pet changes colour less rapidly. You could also change the colours in the list to ones you like better, or add extra colours.

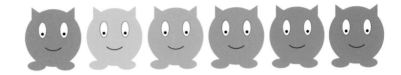

Feed me!

Pets need food, as well as stroking and tickling. Can you figure out ways to feed your pet and keep it healthy?

A growing Screen Pet needs plenty of healthy food to eat!

1 Perhaps try adding a "Feed me!" button to Screen Pet's window and a `feed()` function that's called when you click the button.

2 You could even make Screen Pet grow if you click "Feed me!" a certain number of times. This line of code makes its body bigger.

This code reshapes the oval that makes up Screen Pet's body.

```
body = c.create_oval(15, 20, 395, 350, outline=c.body_color, fill=c.body_color)
```

3 Then try writing some code so that your pet's body shrinks back to its original size again if it doesn't get enough food.

▷ **Clean that up!**
The problem with feeding Screen Pet is that it will need to poo as well! Write some code that makes it poo a while after you feed it. Then add a "Clean up" button. Clicking "Clean up" should call a handler function that removes the poo.

A bigger window

If you add buttons or other extra features to Screen Pet's window, it might get a bit crowded and uncomfortable for your pet. If so, you can enlarge the `Tkinter` window. To do this, change the values for width and height in the command that creates the canvas at the start of the main program.

Games in Python

Caterpillar

If all this coding has worked up your appetite, you're not alone – the star of this project is a hungry caterpillar. Using Python's `turtle` module, you'll find out how to animate game characters and control them on screen with the keyboard.

> Maybe it's time you turned over a new leaf!

What happens

You use the four arrow keys to steer a caterpillar around the screen and make it "eat" leaves. Each leaf gives you a point, but it also makes the caterpillar bigger and faster, making the game harder. Keep the caterpillar inside the game window, or it's game over!

Your score is displayed at the top of the game window.

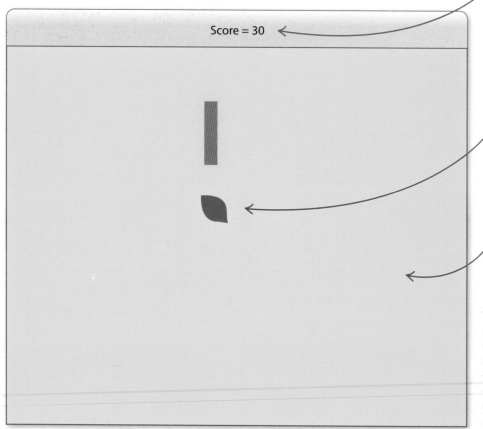

Score = 30

The leaf disappears when eaten, and a new leaf then appears elsewhere.

To start the game, the player has to click on the screen first and then press the space-bar.

◁ **Increasing difficulty**
The more leaves the caterpillar eats, the harder the game becomes. As the caterpillar gets longer and faster, your reactions have to speed up too, otherwise your caterpillar will zoom off the screen.

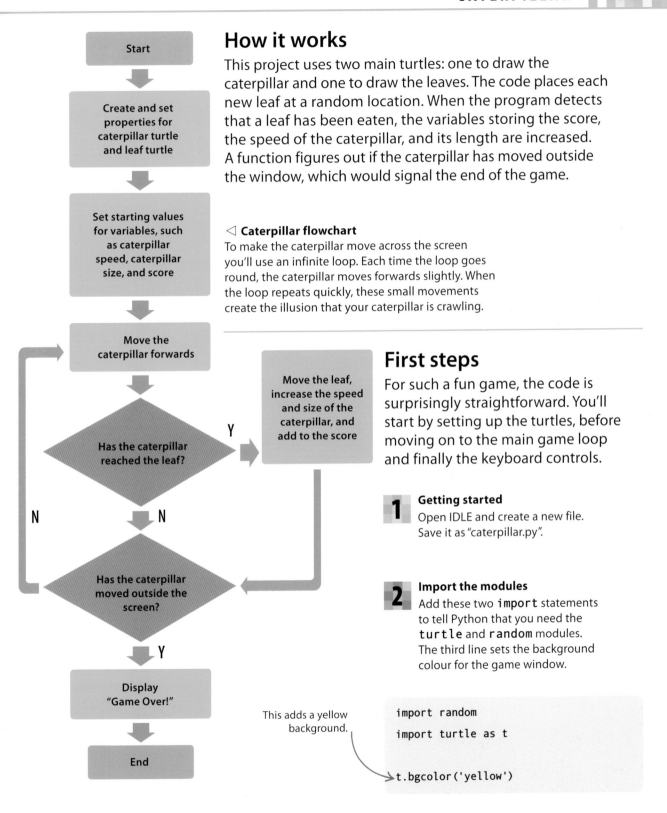

How it works

This project uses two main turtles: one to draw the caterpillar and one to draw the leaves. The code places each new leaf at a random location. When the program detects that a leaf has been eaten, the variables storing the score, the speed of the caterpillar, and its length are increased. A function figures out if the caterpillar has moved outside the window, which would signal the end of the game.

◁ **Caterpillar flowchart**
To make the caterpillar move across the screen you'll use an infinite loop. Each time the loop goes round, the caterpillar moves forwards slightly. When the loop repeats quickly, these small movements create the illusion that your caterpillar is crawling.

First steps

For such a fun game, the code is surprisingly straightforward. You'll start by setting up the turtles, before moving on to the main game loop and finally the keyboard controls.

1 Getting started
Open IDLE and create a new file. Save it as "caterpillar.py".

2 Import the modules
Add these two `import` statements to tell Python that you need the `turtle` and `random` modules. The third line sets the background colour for the game window.

This adds a yellow background.

```
import random
import turtle as t

t.bgcolor('yellow')
```

Flowchart

- Start
- Create and set properties for caterpillar turtle and leaf turtle
- Set starting values for variables, such as caterpillar speed, caterpillar size, and score
- Move the caterpillar forwards
- Has the caterpillar reached the leaf? — Y → Move the leaf, increase the speed and size of the caterpillar, and add to the score
- N → Has the caterpillar moved outside the screen?
  - N → (back to Move the caterpillar forwards)
  - Y → Display "Game Over!"
- End

3 **Create a caterpillar turtle**

Now create the turtle that will become your caterpillar. Add the code shown here. It creates the turtle and sets its colour, shape, and speed. The function `caterpillar.penup()` disables the turtle's pen, allowing you to move the turtle around the screen without drawing a line along the way.

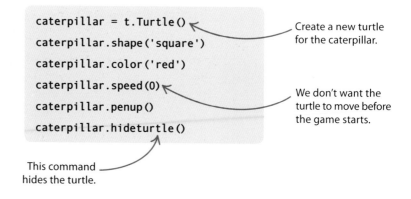

```
caterpillar = t.Turtle()
caterpillar.shape('square')
caterpillar.color('red')
caterpillar.speed(0)
caterpillar.penup()
caterpillar.hideturtle()
```

Create a new turtle for the caterpillar.

We don't want the turtle to move before the game starts.

This command hides the turtle.

4 **Create a leaf turtle**

Below the code for Step 3, type these lines to set up the second turtle, which will draw the leaves. The code uses a list of six coordinate pairs to draw a leaf shape. Once you tell the turtle about this shape, it can reuse the details to draw more leaves. A call to `hideturtle` here makes this turtle invisible on the screen.

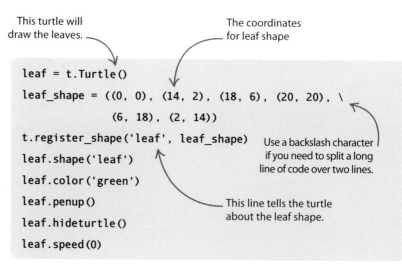

This turtle will draw the leaves.

The coordinates for leaf shape

```
leaf = t.Turtle()
leaf_shape = ((0, 0), (14, 2), (18, 6), (20, 20), \
              (6, 18), (2, 14))
t.register_shape('leaf', leaf_shape)
leaf.shape('leaf')
leaf.color('green')
leaf.penup()
leaf.hideturtle()
leaf.speed(0)
```

Use a backslash character if you need to split a long line of code over two lines.

This line tells the turtle about the leaf shape.

5 **Add some text**

Now set up two more turtles to add text to the game. One will display a message before the action starts, telling players to press space-bar to begin. The other will write the score in the corner of the window. Add these lines after the leaf turtle code.

You'll need to know later if the game has started.

```
game_started = False
text_turtle = t.Turtle()
text_turtle.write('Press SPACE to start', align='center',\
                  font=('Arial', 16, 'bold'))
text_turtle.hideturtle()

score_turtle = t.Turtle()
score_turtle.hideturtle()
score_turtle.speed(0)
```

This line draws some text on the screen.

This hides the turtle but not the text.

Add a turtle to write the score.

The turtle needs to stay where it is, so that it can update the score.

Main loop

Your turtles are now set up and ready to go. Let's write the code that makes the game come to life.

Pass

In Python, if you're not yet sure what code you want inside a function, you can just type in the **pass** keyword and then come back to it later. It's a bit like passing on a question in a quiz.

6 **Placeholder functions**

You can put off defining a function until later by using the **pass** keyword. Under the code for the turtles, add the following placeholders for functions that you'll fill with code in later steps.

```python
def outside_window():
    pass

def game_over():
    pass

def display_score(current_score):
    pass

def place_leaf():
    pass
```

To get a basic version of the program running sooner, you can use placeholders for functions that you'll finish coding later.

7 **Game starter**

After the four placeholder functions comes the **start_game()** function, which sets up some variables and prepares the screen before the main animation loop begins. You'll add the code for the main loop, which forms the rest of this function, in the next step.

The turtle stretches into a caterpillar shape.

```python
def start_game():
    global game_started
    if game_started:
        return
    game_started = True

    score = 0
    text_turtle.clear()

    caterpillar_speed = 2
    caterpillar_length = 3
    caterpillar.shapesize(1, caterpillar_length, 1)
    caterpillar.showturtle()
    display_score(score)
    place_leaf()
```

If the game has already started, the return command makes the function quit so it doesn't run a second time.

Clear the text from the screen.

This line places the first leaf the on screen.

8 Get moving

The main loop moves the caterpillar forwards slightly, before performing two checks. It first checks if the caterpillar has reached the leaf. If the leaf has been eaten, the score increases, a new leaf gets drawn, and the caterpillar gets longer and faster. The loop then checks if the caterpillar has left the window – if so, the game's over. Add the main loop below the code you typed in Step 7.

The very hungry what? No, I've never heard of him!

```
place_leaf()

while True:
    caterpillar.forward(caterpillar_speed)
    if caterpillar.distance(leaf) < 20:
        place_leaf()
        caterpillar_length = caterpillar_length + 1
        caterpillar.shapesize(1, caterpillar_length, 1)
        caterpillar_speed = caterpillar_speed + 1
        score = score + 10
        display_score(score)
    if outside_window():
        game_over()
        break
```

The caterpillar eats the leaf when it's less than 20 pixels away.

The current leaf has been eaten, so add a new leaf.

This will make the caterpillar grow longer.

9 Bind and listen

Now put these lines below the function you've just created. The **onkey()** function binds the space-bar to **start_game()**, so you can delay the start until the player presses space. The **listen()** function allows the program to receive signals from the keyboard.

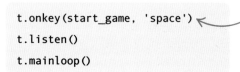

```
t.onkey(start_game, 'space')
t.listen()
t.mainloop()
```

When you press the space-bar, the game begins.

10 Test your code

Run the program. If your code is correct, you should see the caterpillar moving after you press the space-bar. Eventually, it should crawl off the screen. If the program doesn't work, check your code carefully for bugs.

My caterpillar crawled off the screen and into the garden!

Filling in the blanks

It's time to replace **pass** in the placeholder functions with actual code. After adding the code for each function, run the game to see what difference it makes.

11 **Stay inside**

Fill the **outside_window()** function with this code. First it calculates the position of each of the walls. Then it asks the caterpillar for its current position. By comparing the caterpillar's coordinates with the coordinates of the walls, it can tell whether the caterpillar has left the window. Run the program to check the function works – the caterpillar should stop when it reaches the edge.

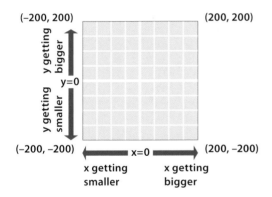

(−200, 200)   (200, 200)

y getting bigger
y=0
y getting smaller

(−200, −200)   x=0   (200, −200)

x getting smaller   x getting bigger

```
def outside_window():
    left_wall = -t.window_width() / 2
    right_wall = t.window_width() / 2
    top_wall = t.window_height() / 2
    bottom_wall = -t.window_height() / 2
    (x, y) = caterpillar.pos()
    outside = \
            x< left_wall or \
            x> right_wall or \
            y< bottom_wall or \
            y> top_wall
    return outside
```

This function returns two values (a "tuple").

If any of the four conditions above is **True**, then **outside = True**.

◁ **How it works**

The centre of the window has the coordinates (0, 0). Since the window is 400 wide, the right wall is half the width from the centre, which is 200. The code gets the left wall's position by subtracting half the width from 0. In other words, 0 – 200, which is −200. It finds the position of the top and bottom walls by a similar method.

12 **GAME OVER!**

Now you know when the caterpillar has left the screen, display a message to tell the player the game has ended. Fill in the **game_over()** function with this code. When called, the function will hide the caterpillar and leaf, and write "GAME OVER!" on the screen.

```
def game_over():
    caterpillar.color('yellow')
    leaf.color('yellow')
    t.penup()
    t.hideturtle()
    t.write('GAME OVER!', align='center', font=('Arial', 30, 'normal'))
```

The text should be centred (Python uses the US spelling "center".)

13

Show the score
The function `display_score()` instructs the score turtle to rewrite the score, putting the latest total on the screen. This function is called whenever the caterpillar reaches a leaf.

```python
def display_score(current_score):
    score_turtle.clear()
    score_turtle.penup()
    x = (t.window_width() / 2) - 50
    y = (t.window_height() / 2) - 50
    score_turtle.setpos(x, y)
    score_turtle.write(str(current_score), align='right', \
                       font=('Arial', 40, 'bold'))
```

50 pixels from the right

50 pixels from the top

14

A new leaf
When a leaf is reached, the function `place_leaf()` is called to move the leaf to a new, random location. It chooses two random numbers between –200 and 200. These numbers become the x and y coordinates for the next leaf.

ht is short for hideturtle.

```python
def place_leaf():
    leaf.ht()
    leaf.setx(random.randint(-200, 200))
    leaf.sety(random.randint(-200, 200))
    leaf.st()
```

Chooses random coordinates to move the leaf.

st is short for showturtle.

15

Turning the caterpillar
Next, to connect the keyboard keys to the caterpillar, add four new direction functions after the `start_game()` function. To make this game a little trickier, the caterpillar can only make 90-degree turns. As a result, each function first checks to see which way the caterpillar is moving before altering its course. If the caterpillar's going the wrong way, the function uses `setheading()` to make it face the right direction.

```python
        game_over()
        break

def move_up():
    if caterpillar.heading() == 0 or caterpillar.heading() == 180:
        caterpillar.setheading(90)

def move_down():
    if caterpillar.heading() == 0 or caterpillar.heading() == 180:
        caterpillar.setheading(270)

def move_left():
    if caterpillar.heading() == 90 or caterpillar.heading() == 270:
        caterpillar.setheading(180)

def move_right():
    if caterpillar.heading() == 90 or caterpillar.heading() == 270:
        caterpillar.setheading(0)
```

Check if the caterpillar is heading left or right.

A heading of 270 sends the caterpillar down the screen.

16 **Listening for presses**
Finally, use **onkey ()** to link the direction functions to the keyboard keys. Add these lines after the **onkey ()** call you made in Step 9. With the steering code in place, the game's complete. Have fun playing and finding out your highest score!

```
t.onkey(start_game, 'space')
t.onkey(move_up, 'Up')
t.onkey(move_right, 'Right')
t.onkey(move_down, 'Down')
t.onkey(move_left, 'Left')
t.listen()
```

Call the **move_up** function when the "up" key is pressed.

Hacks and tweaks

Now that your caterpillar game is working, it won't be too difficult to modify it or even introduce a helper or rival caterpillar!

I'm going to create a giant caterpillar crossed with an enormous turtle...

Make it a two-player game

By creating a second caterpillar turtle with separate keyboard controls, you and a friend can work together to make the caterpillar eat even more leaves!

1 **Create a new caterpillar**
First you'll need to add a new caterpillar. Type these lines near the top of your program, below the code that creates the first caterpillar.

```
caterpillar2 = t.Turtle()
caterpillar2.color('blue')
caterpillar2.shape('square')
caterpillar2.penup()
caterpillar2.speed(0)
caterpillar2.hideturtle()
```

2 **Add a parameter**
To reuse the **outside_window ()** function for both caterpillars, add a parameter to it. Now you can tell it which caterpillar you want it to check on.

```
def outside_window(caterpillar):
```

3 **Hide caterpillar2**
When the **game_over ()** function is called, it hides the first caterpillar. Let's add a line to hide the second caterpillar as well.

```
def game_over():
    caterpillar.color('yellow')
    caterpillar2.color('yellow')
    leaf.color('yellow')
```

4 Change the main function

You'll need to add code for caterpillar2 to the main `start_game()` function. First set its starting shape and make it face the opposite direction to the first caterpillar. Then add it to the `while` loop to make it move, and add a check to the `if` statement so it can eat the leaves. You'll also need to add a line to make it grow. Finally, edit the call to the `outside_window()` function in your second `if` statement to see if the game is over.

```python
    score = 0
    text_turtle.clear()

    caterpillar_speed = 2
    caterpillar_length = 3
    caterpillar.shapesize(1, caterpillar_length, 1)
    caterpillar.showturtle()
    caterpillar2.shapesize(1, caterpillar_length, 1)
    caterpillar2.setheading(180)
    caterpillar2.showturtle()
    display_score(score)
    place_leaf()

    while True:
        caterpillar.forward(caterpillar_speed)
        caterpillar2.forward(caterpillar_speed)
        if caterpillar.distance(leaf) < 20 or leaf.distance(caterpillar2) < 20:
            place_leaf()
            caterpillar_length = caterpillar_length + 1
            caterpillar.shapesize(1, caterpillar_length, 1)
            caterpillar2.shapesize(1, caterpillar_length, 1)
            caterpillar_speed = caterpillar_speed + 1
            score = score + 10
            display_score(score)
        if outside_window(caterpillar) or outside_window(caterpillar2):
            game_over()
```

This sets caterpillar2's starting shape.

Caterpillar2 starts heading left.

Each time the program loops, caterpillar2 moves forwards.

This checks if caterpillar2 has eaten the leaf.

Caterpillar2 gets longer.

Has caterpillar2 left the screen?

5 **Extra controls**

Now assign the keys that the second player will use to control the new caterpillar. The code here uses "w" for up, "a" for left, "s" for down, and "d" for right, but feel free to try out different choices. You'll need four new functions and four uses of **onkey** to tie the new keys to the new functions.

```
def caterpillar2_move_up():
    if caterpillar2.heading() == 0 or caterpillar2.heading() == 180:
        caterpillar2.setheading(90)


def caterpillar2_move_down():
    if caterpillar2.heading() == 0 or caterpillar2.heading() == 180:
        caterpillar2.setheading(270)


def caterpillar2_move_left():
    if caterpillar2.heading() == 90 or caterpillar2.heading() == 270:
        caterpillar2.setheading(180)


def caterpillar2_move_right():
    if caterpillar2.heading() == 90 or caterpillar2.heading() == 270:
        caterpillar2.setheading(0)


t.onkey(caterpillar2_move_up, 'w')
t.onkey(caterpillar2_move_right, 'd')
t.onkey(caterpillar2_move_down, 's')
t.onkey(caterpillar2_move_left, 'a')
```

That's an old photo of me winning the competition!

△ **Make it competitive**

See if you can figure out how to adapt the two-player game to record each player's score and then declare the winner at the end. Here's a tip: you'll need a new variable to keep track of the second player's score. When a caterpillar eats a leaf, you'll need to add a point only to that caterpillar's score. Finally, when the game is over, you can compare the scores to see who's won.

▽ **Make it harder or easier**

If you alter the values inside the loop that increase the length (+1) and speed (+2) of the caterpillar, you can change the difficulty of the game. Higher numbers will make the game harder, while lower numbers will make it easier.

What I'm doing is way trickier!

Snap

Challenge your friends to a game of digital snap. This fast-paced, two-player game requires a sharp eye and lightning-fast reactions. It works just like the card game but uses coloured shapes that appear on the screen rather than cards that are dealt.

What happens

Different shapes appear on the screen at random in either black, red, green, or blue. If a colour appears twice in succession, hit the snap key. Player 1 presses the "q" key to snap and player 2 the "p" key. Each correct snap scores a point. Snap at the wrong time and you lose a point. The player with the highest score is the winner.

▽ **Starting the game**
This game works in a `Tkinter` window. When you start the program, the `Tkinter` window might be hidden behind IDLE windows on your desktop. Move them out of the way so you can see the game. Be quick though: the snap shapes start appearing 3 seconds after you run the program.

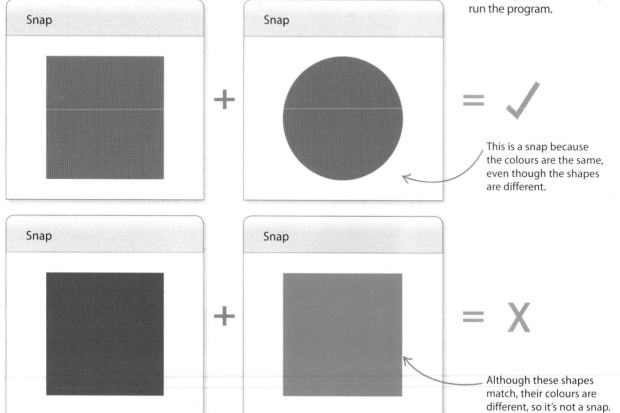

This is a snap because the colours are the same, even though the shapes are different.

Although these shapes match, their colours are different, so it's not a snap.

How it works

This project uses `Tkinter` to create the shapes. `Tkinter`'s `mainloop()` function schedules a function that you'll create to show the next shape. The `random` module's `shuffle()` function makes sure the shapes always appear in a different order. The "q" and "p" keys are bound (linked) to a `snap()` function, so that each time one of these keys is pressed, it updates the relevant player's score.

▷ **Snap flowchart**
The program runs for as long as there are still shapes left to be revealed. It reacts to the key presses of the players when they think they see a snap. When there are no more shapes left, the winner is declared and the game ends.

EXPERT TIPS

Sleep

Computers work a lot faster than you can. Sometimes this causes problems. If you tell a computer to show a shape to the user and then hide it again, without a break, the computer does it so quickly that the person won't see the shape. To fix this, Snap uses the time module's `sleep()` function, which pauses the program for a set number of seconds: `time.sleep(1)`, for example, puts the program to sleep for 1 second before it runs the next line of code.

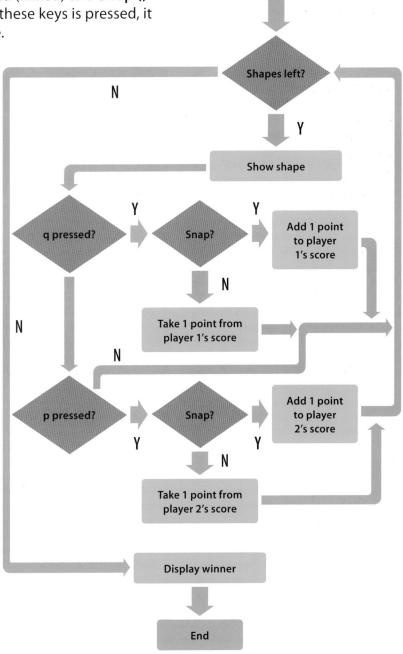

Getting started

First you need to import the relevant modules and create a graphical user interface (GUI). Then you need to create a canvas to draw the shapes on.

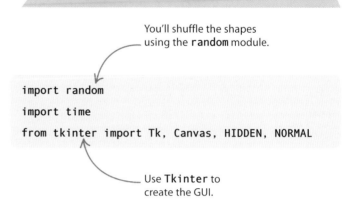

Let's go!

1 **Create a new file**
Open IDLE. Create a new file and save it as "snap.py".

2 **Add modules**
First import the **random** and **time** modules, and parts of **Tkinter**. **Time** lets you create a delay so that the player is able to read a "SNAP!" or "WRONG!" message before the next shape is shown. **HIDDEN** lets you hide each shape until you want to show it with **NORMAL** – otherwise all the shapes will appear on the screen at the start of the game.

You'll shuffle the shapes using the **random** module.

```
import random
import time
from tkinter import Tk, Canvas, HIDDEN, NORMAL
```

Use **Tkinter** to create the GUI.

3 **Set up the GUI**
Now type the code shown here to create a **Tkinter** window (also called a root widget) with the title "Snap". Run the code to check it. The window may be hidden behind the other windows on the desktop.

```
from tkinter import Tk, Canvas, HIDDEN, NORMAL


root = Tk()
root.title('Snap')
```

4 **Create the canvas**
Type this line to create the canvas – the blank space on which the shapes will appear.

```
root.title('Snap')
c = Canvas(root, width=400, height=400)
```

Making the shapes

The next stage is to create the coloured shapes using functions from **Tkinter**'s Canvas widget. You'll draw circles, squares, and rectangles, each in four different colours.

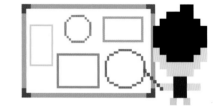

5 **Make a store for the shapes**
You need to make a list so that you can store all the shapes somewhere. Add this line at the bottom of your file.

```
c = Canvas(root, width=400, height=400)


shapes = []
```

6 Create the circles

To draw a circle, use the Canvas widget's `create_oval()` function. Type the following code below the shapes list. It creates four circles of the same size – one each in black, red, green, and blue – and adds them to the shapes list.

Set the state to **HIDDEN** so that the shape doesn't appear on the screen when the program starts. It has to wait its turn.

Don't forget to save your work.

These are the (x0, y0) coordinates (see box).

These are the (x1, y1) coordinates (see box).

```
shapes = []

circle = c.create_oval(35, 20, 365, 350, outline='black', fill='black', state=HIDDEN)
shapes.append(circle)
circle = c.create_oval(35, 20, 365, 350, outline='red', fill='red', state=HIDDEN)
shapes.append(circle)
circle = c.create_oval(35, 20, 365, 350, outline='green', fill='green', state=HIDDEN)
shapes.append(circle)
circle = c.create_oval(35, 20, 365, 350, outline='blue', fill='blue', state=HIDDEN)
shapes.append(circle)
c.pack()
```

This line puts the shapes onto the canvas. Without it, none of the shapes would be displayed.

The circle's colour is determined by `outline` and `fill`.

 EXPERT TIPS

Create ovals

The `create.oval()` function draws an oval as if it's inside an invisible box. The four numbers within the brackets decide the position of the circles on the screen. They are the coordinates of two opposing corners of the box. The greater the difference between the two pairs of numbers, the bigger the circle.

The first pair of numbers (x0, y0) shows the position of the box's top-left corner.

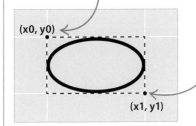

(x0, y0)

(x1, y1) shows the position of the bottom-right corner.

(x1, y1)

7 Show the circles

Try running the program. Do you see any shapes? Remember that you set their states to **HIDDEN**. Change one shape's state to **NORMAL** and run the code again. You should now be able to see that shape on the screen. Be careful not to set more than one shape to **NORMAL**. If you do, they'll all show at once, drawn one on top of the other.

I tried blowing bubbles, but I've blown circles!

8 Add some rectangles

Now create four different-coloured rectangles using **Canvas**'s **create_rectangle()** function. Insert this block of code between the circle-drawing code and **c.pack()**. To avoid typing it all out, just type the first two lines, then copy and paste them three times and change the colours.

Don't forget to save your work.

```
shapes.append(circle)

rectangle = c.create_rectangle(35, 100, 365, 270, outline='black', fill='black', state=HIDDEN)
shapes.append(rectangle)
rectangle = c.create_rectangle(35, 100, 365, 270, outline='red', fill='red', state=HIDDEN)
shapes.append(rectangle)
rectangle = c.create_rectangle(35, 100, 365, 270, outline='green', fill='green', state=HIDDEN)
shapes.append(rectangle)
rectangle = c.create_rectangle(35, 100, 365, 270, outline='blue', fill='blue', state=HIDDEN)
shapes.append(rectangle)

c.pack()
```

9 Add some squares

Next draw the squares. You can use the same function that you used to create the rectangles, but this time you'll turn the rectangles into squares by making all their sides the same length. Add this block of code between the rectangle code and **c.pack()**.

```
shapes.append(rectangle)

square = c.create_rectangle(35, 20, 365, 350, outline='black', fill='black', state=HIDDEN)
shapes.append(square)
square = c.create_rectangle(35, 20, 365, 350, outline='red', fill='red', state=HIDDEN)
shapes.append(square)
square = c.create_rectangle(35, 20, 365, 350, outline='green', fill='green', state=HIDDEN)
shapes.append(square)
square = c.create_rectangle(35, 20, 365, 350, outline='blue', fill='blue', state=HIDDEN)
shapes.append(square)

c.pack()
```

10 **Shuffle the shapes**
To ensure that the shapes don't appear in the same order each time, you need to shuffle them – just like you would do with a pack of cards. The `shuffle()` function in `random` can do this for you. Insert this line after `c.pack()`.

```
random.shuffle(shapes)
```

Getting ready

In the next part of the build, you'll set up several variables and write a few bits of code that get the game ready for playing. However, it won't work until we add the functions in the last stage.

Are you ready for the game?

EXPERT TIPS

Nothing really matters

Coders often need to set up variables with a starting value of zero, such as the scores in this game. But how do you do this if a variable holds a string rather than a number? The answer is to use a pair of quote marks with nothing between them. Some variables, however, don't have an obvious default value such as 0 or an empty string. In that case, you can use the word "None", as we do below.

The **shape** variable has no value yet.

11 **Set up variables**
You'll need variables to keep track of various things while the program is running, including the current shape, the previous and current colour, and the two players' scores.

Neither player has any points at the start, so the value of both is set to 0.

```
random.shuffle(shapes)

shape = None
previous_color = ''
current_color = ''
player1_score = 0
player2_score = 0
```

The **color** variables hold an empty string.

12 **Add a delay**
Now add a line to create a 3-second delay before the first shape appears. This gives the player time to find the `Tkinter` window in case it's hidden behind other windows on the desktop. You'll create the `next_shape()` function later, in Steps 16 and 17.

```
player2_score = 0

root.after(3000, next_shape)
```

The program waits for 3,000 milliseconds, or 3 seconds before showing the next shape.

13 React to snaps

Next add these two lines to your code. The **bind()** function tells the GUI to listen for the "q" or "p" key being pressed, and to call the **snap()** function each time it happens. You'll create the **snap()** function later.

```
root.after(3000, next_shape)
c.bind('q', snap)
c.bind('p', snap)
```

14 Send key presses to the GUI

The **focus_set()** function tells the key presses to go to the canvas. The GUI wouldn't react to "q" and "p" being pressed without this function being called. Type this line below the **bind()** function calls.

```
c.bind('q', snap)
c.bind('p', snap)
c.focus_set()
```

15 Start the main loop

Add this line right at the end of your file. Once we add the **next_shape()** and **snap()** functions, the main loop will update the GUI with the next shape and listen for key presses.

```
c.focus_set()


root.mainloop()
```

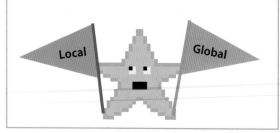
Coding the functions

The last stage is to create two functions: one to show the next shape, and another to handle snaps. Type them at the top of your program, just below the import statements.

16 Create the function

The **next_shape()** function shows the coloured shapes one after another, like cards being dealt. Start defining the function by typing the code below. It labels some of your variables as global (see box, left) and updates **previous_color**.

Using the **global** keyword ensures that changes to the variables are seen throughout the program.

```
def next_shape():
    global shape
    global previous_color
    global current_color
```

This line sets **previous_color** to **current_color** before the code gets the next shape.

```
    previous_color = current_color
```

17 **Complete the function**
Now type out of the rest of the function. To show a new shape, we
need to change its state from HIDDEN to NORMAL. The code below
does this by using **Canvas**'s **itemconfigure()** function. It uses
another Canvas function, **itemcget()**, to update the **current_
color** variable, which will be used to check for a snap.

```
previous_color = current_color

c.delete(shape)

if len(shapes) > 0:
    shape = shapes.pop()
    c.itemconfigure(shape, state=NORMAL)
    current_color = c.itemcget(shape, 'fill')
    root.after(1000, next_shape)
else:
    c.unbind('q')
    c.unbind('p')
    if player1_score > player2_score:
        c.create_text(200, 200, text='Winner: Player 1')
    elif player2_score > player1_score:
        c.create_text(200, 200, text='Winner: Player 2')
    else:
        c.create_text(200, 200, text='Draw')
    c.pack()
```

Delete the current shape, so that the
next shape doesn't show on top of it
and so that it won't be shown again.

Get the next shape if
there are any shapes left.

Make the new shape visible.

Assign **current_color** to
the colour of the new shape.

Wait 1 second before
showing the next shape.

These lines stop the program
responding to snaps after
the game is over.

This code shows the
winner on the screen or
declares the game a draw.

Configuring Canvas items

You can alter things that appear on the Canvas by
using **Canvas**'s **itemconfigure()** function. In
this game, for instance, you use **itemconfigure()**
to change shapes from hidden to visible, but you
could also use it to change their colour or other
characteristics. To use **itemconfigure()**, put the
name of the item you want to change in brackets,
followed by a comma and then the characteristic
and its new value.

The characteristic
being changed

```
c.itemconfigure(shape, state=NORMAL)
```

The name of the
Canvas item you
want to change.

The new
value

18 **Is it a snap?**
To complete the game, create your last function: **snap()**. This function will check which player has hit their key and whether the snap is valid (correct). It will then update the scores and show a message. Add this code beneath the **next_shape()** function.

Don't forget to save
your work.

```python
def snap(event):
    global shape
    global player1_score
    global player2_score
    valid = False

    c.delete(shape)

    if previous_color == current_color:
        valid = True

    if valid:
        if event.char == 'q':
            player1_score = player1_score + 1
        else:
            player2_score = player2_score + 1
        shape = c.create_text(200, 200, text='SNAP! You score 1 point!')
    else:
        if event.char == 'q':
            player1_score = player1_score - 1
        else:
            player2_score = player2_score - 1
        shape = c.create_text(200, 200, text='WRONG! You lose 1 point!')
    c.pack()
    root.update_idletasks()
    time.sleep(1)
```

Label these variables as global so the function can change them.

Check if it's a valid snap (if the colour of the previous shape matches the colour of the current shape).

If the snap is valid, check which player snapped and add 1 to their score.

This line shows a message when a player makes a valid snap.

Otherwise (**else**), take away one point from the player that snapped.

This line shows a message when a player snaps at the wrong time.

This line forces the program to update the GUI with the snap message immediately.

Wait 1 second while players read the message.

19 **Test your code**
Now run the program to check it works. Remember you need to click on the **Tkinter** window before it will respond to the "q" and "p" keys.

Hacks and tweaks

Tkinter can show lots of different colours and shapes besides circles, squares, and rectangles, so there's plenty of scope to customize your game. Here are some ideas to try out – including making the game cheat-proof!

△ **Coloured outlines**
The program looks at the **fill** parameter, not the **outline**, when it's judging whether a valid snap has been made. You can give different-coloured outlines to shapes and they will still make a snap so long as their fill colours match.

▽ **Speed up the game**
You can make the game a bit harder by reducing the time delay between each shape as the game progresses. Hint: try storing the time in a variable, starting at 1000 and subtracting 25 from it each time a shape is shown. These numbers are just suggestions – experiment with them to see what you think works best.

Speed up!

I'll try, but I'm feeling a bit sluggish!

△ **Add more colours**
You may have noticed that Snap is quite a short game. To make it longer, add extra squares, rectangles, and circles using different colours.

Make new shapes

You can change the parameters of **create_oval ()** to produce an oval rather than a circle. **Tkinter** can also draw arcs, lines, and polygons. Try out the examples shown here, and play around with the parameters. Remember to keep the **state** as **HIDDEN** to hide the shape until it's time to show it.

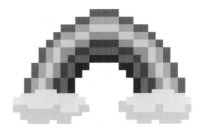

1 **Draw arcs**
Use the **create_arc ()** function to draw arcs. A solid arc is drawn unless you give your arc a style. To use **Tkinter**'s different arc styles, import **CHORD** and **ARC** by changing the third line of your program, as shown below. Then add some chords and arcs to your list of shapes, as shown overleaf.

Wow! I wonder who drew that arc?

Type this to import the arc styles.

```
from tkinter import Tk, Canvas, HIDDEN, NORMAL, CHORD, ARC
```

```
arc = c.create_arc(-235, 120, 365, 370, outline='black', \
                 fill='black', state=HIDDEN)
```

This arc is drawn in full, as it hasn't been given a style.

```
arc = c.create_arc(-235, 120, 365, 370, outline='red', \
                 fill='red', state=HIDDEN, style=CHORD)
```

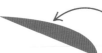

The style CHORD shows a slice across the arc.

```
arc = c.create_arc(-235, 120, 365, 370, outline='green', \
                 fill='green', state=HIDDEN, style=ARC)
```

The style ARC shows just the outer curve.

2 Draw lines

Now try adding some lines to your list of shapes using the **create_line()** function.

```
line = c.create_line(35, 200, 365, 200, fill='blue', state=HIDDEN)
```

```
line = c.create_line(35, 20, 365, 350, fill='black', state=HIDDEN)
```

3 Draw polygons

Next try making some polygons for your shape collection, using **create_polygon()**. You'll need to give coordinates for each corner of your polygons.

The three pairs of numbers in the code give the coordinates of the triangle's corners.

```
polygon = c.create_polygon(35, 200, 365, 200, 200, 35,
outline='blue', fill='blue', state=HIDDEN)
```

Stop players cheating

Right now, if a snap is valid and both players hit their snap keys at the same time, they each get a point. In fact, they will still be able to score points up until the next shape is shown, since the previous and current colour will still be the same. Try this hack to stop the players cheating.

1 Go global

First you need to say that **previous_color** is a global variable in the **snap()** function, because you need to change its value. Add this line under the other global variables.

```
global previous_color
```

2 **Block a multiple snap**

Next add the following line to the **snap()** function to set the value of **previous_color** to the empty string (' ') after a correct snap. Now if a player presses their key again before the next shape is shown, they will lose a point. This is because '' will never be equal to the current colour, except before the first shape is shown.

There's nothing I don't know about multiple snaps!

```
        shape = c.create_text(200, 200, text='SNAP! You scored 1 point!'
    previous_color = ''
```

3 **Prevent early snaps**

Since **previous_color** and **current_color** are equal at the beginning of the game, players can still cheat by pressing their key before the first shape appears. To solve this, set the two variables to different strings at the start. Change their values to "a" and "b".

```
previous_color = 'a'
current_color = 'b'
```

Starting with different strings means that a snap can't be made until the shapes appear on the screen.

4 **Change the messages**

If both players press their keys at almost the same time, it might be confusing as to who has scored or lost a point. To fix this, you can change the messages that are displayed when players attempt a snap.

Don't forget to save your work.

```
if valid:
    if event.char == 'q':
        player1_score = player1_score + 1
        shape = c.create_text(200, 200, text='SNAP! Player 1 scores 1 point!')
    else:
        player2_score = player2_score + 1
        shape = c.create_text(200, 200, text='SNAP! Player 2 scores 1 point!')
    previous_color = ''
else:
    if event.char == 'q':
        player1_score = player1_score - 1
        shape = c.create_text(200, 200, text='WRONG! Player 1 lost 1 point!')
    else:
        player2_score = player2_score - 1
        shape = c.create_text(200, 200, text='WRONG! Player 2 lost 1 point!')
```

Matchmaker

How good is your memory? Put it to the test in this fun game where you have to find pairs of matching symbols. See how quickly you can find all 12 matching pairs!

Have you got a good memory?

I can't remember!

What happens

When you run the program, it opens a window showing a grid of buttons. Click on them in pairs to reveal the hidden symbols. If two symbols are the same, you've found a match and the symbols remain visible on the screen. Otherwise, the two buttons are reset. Try to remember the location of each hidden symbol to quickly find all the pairs.

The grid shows 24 buttons arranged into four rows of six.

Matchmaker

✈

✊

✊

✈

✓

✌

✌

✓

Click on a button to reveal a symbol.

There are only two of each symbol.

◁ **GUI window**
The grid window is a graphical user interface (GUI) created by Python's **Tkinter** module.

If you make a wrong match, the symbols are hidden again.

Matching symbols are left showing on the grid.

How it works

This project uses the `Tkinter` module to display the button grid. `Tkinter`'s `mainloop()` function listens for button presses and handles them with a special kind of function, called a `lambda` function, that reveals a symbol. If an unmatched symbol has already been revealed, the program checks to see if the second one matches. The project stores the buttons in a dictionary and the symbols in a list.

▽ **Matchmaker flowchart**
After shuffling the symbols and creating the grid, the program spends its time listening for button presses. It ends when all the matching pairs have been found.

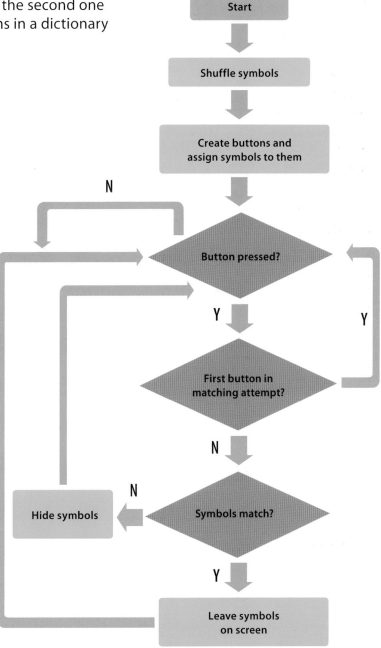

I've found a matching pear!

Getting started

In the first part of the project, you'll set up the graphical user interface (GUI) and add the pairs of symbols that will be hidden by the buttons.

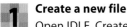

I suppose I'd better get started!

1 Create a new file
Open IDLE. Create a new file and save it as "matchmaker.py".

File

Save

Save As

DISABLED stops a button from responding after its symbol has been matched.

2 Add modules
Now type this code at the top of your file to import the modules you need for this project. You'll use **random** to shuffle the symbols, **time** to pause the program, and **Tkinter** to create the GUI.

```
import random
import time
from tkinter import Tk, Button, DISABLED
```

Button creates the buttons in the Tkinter window.

These lines create a Tkinter window and give it a title.

3 Set up the GUI
Under the import commands, add this code, which will set up the GUI. The **root.resizable()** function prevents the player from resizing the window. This is important, since changing the size of the window will mess up the button layout that you'll create later on.

```
root = Tk()
root.title('Matchmaker')
root.resizable(width=False, height=False)
```

This line keeps the window at its original size.

4 Test your code
Now run the code. You should see an empty **Tkinter** window with the heading "Matchmaker". If you can't see it, it's probably hidden behind other windows.

Matchmaker

Don't forget to save your work.

5 Make some variables

Under the code for Step 3, add the variables that the program needs, and create a dictionary to store the buttons in. For each attempt at a match, you need to remember whether it's the first or second symbol in the match. You also need to keep track of the first button press so you can compare it with the second button press.

```
root.resizable(width=False, height=False)

buttons = {}

first = True

previousX = 0

previousY = 0
```

This is the dictionary.

This variable is used to check if the symbol is the first in the match.

These two variables keep track of the last button pressed.

6 Add the symbols

Next type the code below to add the symbols the game will use. As in the Nine Lives project, the program uses Unicode characters. There are 12 pairs, making 24 in total. Add this code under the variables added in Step 5.

 U+2702   U+2705   U+2708   U+2709

 U+270A   U+270B   U+270C   U+270F

 U+2712   U+2714   U+2716   U+2728

```
previousY = 0

button_symbols = {}

symbols = [u'\u2702', u'\u2702', u'\u2705', u'\u2705', u'\u2708', u'\u2708',
           u'\u2709', u'\u2709', u'\u270A', u'\u270A', u'\u270B', u'\u270B',
           u'\u270C', u'\u270C', u'\u270F', u'\u270F', u'\u2712', u'\u2712',
           u'\u2714', u'\u2714', u'\u2716', u'\u2716', u'\u2728', u'\u2728']
```

The symbol for each button is stored in this dictionary.

This list stores the 12 pairs of symbols that will be used in the game.

The **shuffle()** function from the **random** module mixes up the shapes.

7 Shuffle the symbols

You don't want the symbols to appear in the same place every time. After several games, the player would remember their positions and would be able to match them all at first attempt, every time. To prevent this, you need to shuffle the symbols before each game starts. Add this line after the list of symbols.

```
random.shuffle(symbols)
```

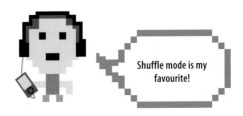

Shuffle mode is my favourite!

Bring on the buttons!

In the next stage you'll make the buttons and add them to the GUI. Then you'll create a function called **show_symbol()** to control what happens when a player clicks on the buttons.

Button

Tkinter has a built-in widget called **Button**, which we use to create the GUI buttons. You can pass different parameters to it. The ones we need are **command**, **width**, and **height**. The **command** parameter tells the program what to do when a button is pressed. This is a function call. In our program, it calls a **lambda** function. The **width** and **height** parameters are used to set the size of the button.

8 **Build the grid**
The grid will consist of 24 buttons arranged into four rows of six. To lay out the grid, you'll use nested loops. The outer x loop will work from left to right across the six columns, while the inner y loop will work from top to bottom down each column. Once the loops have run, each button will have been given a pair of **x** and **y** coordinates that set its position on the grid. Put this block of code after the shuffle command.

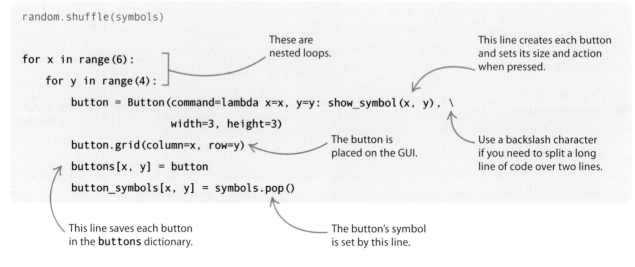

```
random.shuffle(symbols)

for x in range(6):
    for y in range(4):
        button = Button(command=lambda x=x, y=y: show_symbol(x, y), \
                        width=3, height=3)
        button.grid(column=x, row=y)
        buttons[x, y] = button
        button_symbols[x, y] = symbols.pop()
```

These are nested loops.

This line creates each button and sets its size and action when pressed.

The button is placed on the GUI.

Use a backslash character if you need to split a long line of code over two lines.

This line saves each button in the **buttons** dictionary.

The button's symbol is set by this line.

△ How it works

Each time the loop runs, the **lambda** function saves the current button's x and y values (the row and column it's in). When the button is pressed, it calls the **show_symbol()** function (which you'll create later) with these values, so the function knows which button has been pressed and which symbol to reveal.

And now for the big reveal...

.. . REMEMBER

Nested loops

You might remember reading about nested loops on page 35. You can put as many loops inside one another as you want. In this project, the outer loop runs six times. Each time the outer loop runs, the inner loop runs four times. So in total, the inner loop runs 6 x 4 = 24 times.

Oh, look.
A nested loop!

9

Start the main loop

Now start `Tkinter`'s `mainloop`. Once this loop starts, the GUI will be displayed and it will start listening for button presses. Type this line after the code you added in Step 8.

```
button_symbols[x, y] = symbols.pop()


root.mainloop()
```

10

Test your code

Run the program again. Your `Tkinter` window should now be filled with 24 buttons arranged in a grid. If it doesn't look similar to the picture shown here, check your code carefully for any errors.

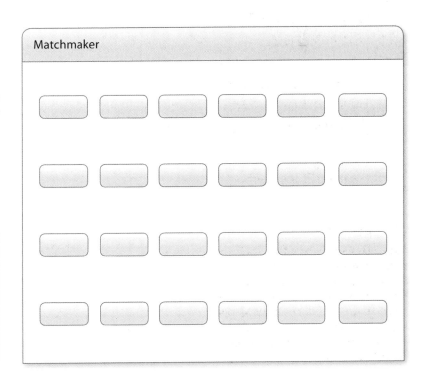

Matchmaker

```
previousX = 0
previousY = 0
```

11 **Show the symbol**

Finally, you need to create the function that handles the button presses. This function will always display a symbol, but how it operates depends on whether it's the first or second turn in the matching attempt. If it's the first turn, the function just needs to remember which button was pressed. If it's the second turn, it needs to check if the symbols match. Symbols that don't match are hidden. Matching symbols are left showing and their buttons are disabled.

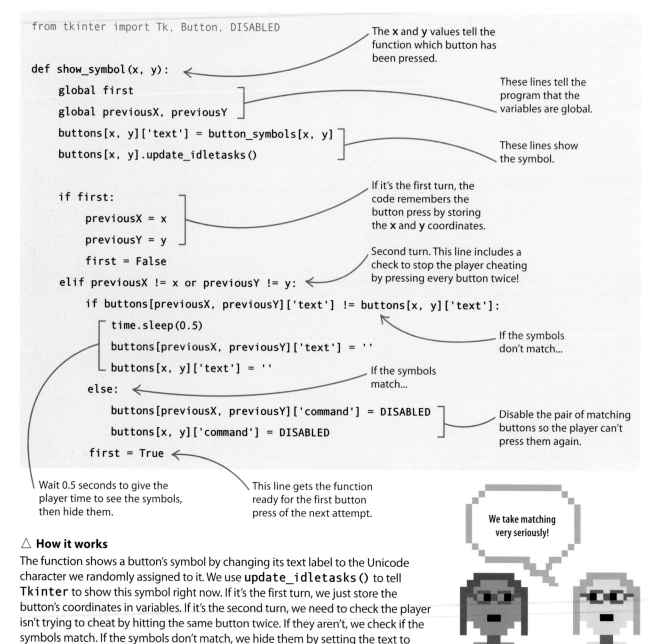

```python
from tkinter import Tk, Button, DISABLED
```
The **x** and **y** values tell the function which button has been pressed.

```python
def show_symbol(x, y):
    global first
    global previousX, previousY
```
These lines tell the program that the variables are global.

```python
    buttons[x, y]['text'] = button_symbols[x, y]
    buttons[x, y].update_idletasks()
```
These lines show the symbol.

```python
    if first:
        previousX = x
        previousY = y
        first = False
```
If it's the first turn, the code remembers the button press by storing the x and y coordinates.

```python
    elif previousX != x or previousY != y:
```
Second turn. This line includes a check to stop the player cheating by pressing every button twice!

```python
        if buttons[previousX, previousY]['text'] != buttons[x, y]['text']:
```
If the symbols don't match...

```python
            time.sleep(0.5)
            buttons[previousX, previousY]['text'] = ''
            buttons[x, y]['text'] = ''
```

```python
        else:
```
If the symbols match...

```python
            buttons[previousX, previousY]['command'] = DISABLED
            buttons[x, y]['command'] = DISABLED
```
Disable the pair of matching buttons so the player can't press them again.

```python
        first = True
```
This line gets the function ready for the first button press of the next attempt.

Wait 0.5 seconds to give the player time to see the symbols, then hide them.

We take matching very seriously!

△ **How it works**

The function shows a button's symbol by changing its text label to the Unicode character we randomly assigned to it. We use **update_idletasks()** to tell **Tkinter** to show this symbol right now. If it's the first turn, we just store the button's coordinates in variables. If it's the second turn, we need to check the player isn't trying to cheat by hitting the same button twice. If they aren't, we check if the symbols match. If the symbols don't match, we hide them by setting the text to empty strings; if they do match, we leave them showing but disable the buttons.

Hacks and tweaks

You could adapt this game in many ways. You can show the number of moves taken to finish the game, so the player can try and beat their own score or challenge their friends. You could also add more symbols to make the game harder.

Show the number of moves

At the moment, the player has no way of knowing how well they've done or if they've done any better than their friends. How can we make the game more competitive? Let's add a variable to count how many turns a player takes to finish the game. Then players can compete to see who gets the lowest score.

Let's make the game more competitive!

1 Add a new module
You need to import **Tkinter**'s **messagebox** widget to display the number of moves at the end of the game. In the import line, add the word **messagebox** after **DISABLED**.

```
from tkinter import Tk, Button, DISABLED, messagebox
```

2 Make new variables
You'll have to make two extra variables for this hack. One variable will keep track of the number of moves the player makes, while the other will remember how many pairs they've found. Give them both a starting value of 0. Put these lines below the variable **previousY**.

The player hasn't made any moves yet, or found any pairs, so the values are 0.

```
previousY = 0
moves = 0
pairs = 0
```

3 Declare them global
The **moves** and **pairs** variables are global variables, and they'll need to be changed by the **show_symbol ()** function. Let **show_symbol ()** know this by putting these two lines near the top of the function.

```
def show_symbol(x, y):
    global first
    global previousX, previousY
    global moves
    global pairs
```

4 **Count the moves**

A move is two button presses (one matching attempt). So you only need to add 1 to the **moves** variable when the **show_symbol()** function is called for the first or the second button press – not for both. Let's do it for the first button press. Change the **show_symbol()** function to look like this.

```
if first:
    previousX = x
    previousY = y
    first = False
    moves = moves + 1
```

5 **Display a message**

Now add the following code near the bottom of the **show_symbol()** function. It will track the matched pairs and show a message box at the end of the game telling the player how many moves they took. When the player clicks the box's OK button, the code calls the **close_window()** function, which we'll add next.

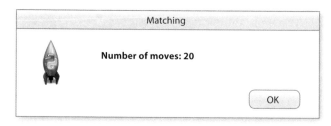

```
    buttons[x, y]['command'] = DISABLED
    pairs = pairs + 1
    if pairs == len(buttons)/2:
        messagebox.showinfo('Matching', 'Number of moves: ' +
                            str(moves), command=close_window)
```

Add 1 to the number of pairs found.

This line displays a box showing the number of moves.

If all the pairs have been found, run the code under this line.

△ **How it works**

There are 12 pairs of symbols, so you could simply have typed **pairs == 12** in the hack. However, your code is smarter than this. It calculates the number of pairs by using **pairs == len(buttons)/2**. This allows you to add more buttons to the game without having to update this bit of code.

6 **Close the window**

Finally, you need to create a **close_window()** function, to make the program exit the game when the player clicks the OK button on the "Number of moves" message box. Add this code under the line that imports the modules.

```
def close_window(self):
    root.destroy()
```

This command closes the window.

Add more buttons

Let's really challenge the player's memory by adding more buttons and symbols to the game.

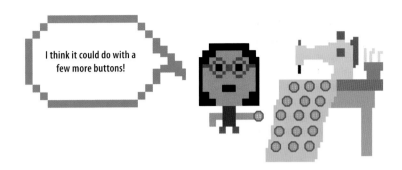

I think it could do with a few more buttons!

1 Extra symbols

First you need to add more pairs to the symbols list. Include this new line in the code.

 U+2733   U+2734   U+2744

```python
symbols = [u'\u2702', u'\u2702', u'\u2705', u'\u2705', u'\u2708', u'\u2708',
           u'\u2709', u'\u2709', u'\u270A', u'\u270A', u'\u270B', u'\u270B',
           u'\u270C', u'\u270C', u'\u270F', u'\u270F', u'\u2712', u'\u2712',
           u'\u2714', u'\u2714', u'\u2716', u'\u2716', u'\u2728', u'\u2728',
           u'\u2733', u'\u2733', u'\u2734', u'\u2734', u'\u2744', u'\u2744']
```

Add the three pairs of new symbols to the end of the list.

2 Extra buttons

Now add an extra row of buttons. To do this, you just need to change the **y** range in the nested loops from 4 to 5, as shown on the right.

```python
for x in range(6):
    for y in range(5):
```

This line will now create five rows of buttons instead of four.

3 Even bigger?

You now have a total of 30 buttons. If you want to add more, make sure that the number of extra buttons you add is a multiple of 6 so that you always add complete rows. If you're feeling adventurous, you could experiment with different button layouts by changing the nested loops.

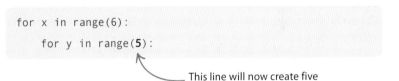

U+2747   U+274C   U+274E   U+2753   U+2754

 U+2755   U+2757   U+2764   U+2795   U+2796

 U+2797   U+27A1   U+27B0

Egg Catcher

This game will test your concentration and the speed of your reflexes. Don't crack under pressure – just catch as many eggs as you can to get a high score. Challenge your friends to see who is the champion egg catcher!

What happens

Move the catcher along the bottom of the screen to catch each egg before it touches the ground. When you scoop up an egg you score points, but if you drop an egg you lose a life. Beware: the more eggs you catch, the more frequently new eggs appear at the top of the screen and the faster they fall. Lose all three lives and the game ends.

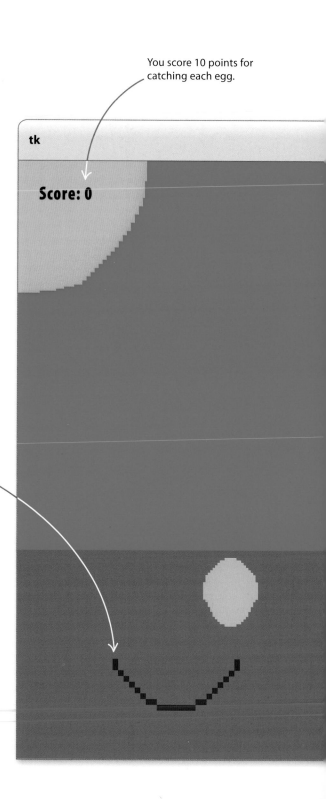

You score 10 points for catching each egg.

Move the catcher to and fro by pressing the left and right arrow keys.

◼ ◼ ▪ EXPERT TIPS

Timing

The timing of the action on the screen is important. At first, a new egg is only added every 4 seconds, otherwise there would be too many eggs. Initially, the eggs move down a little every half second. If the interval was smaller, the game would be too hard. The program checks for a catch once every tenth of a second – any slower, and it might miss it. As the player scores more points, the speed and number of the eggs increases to make the game more challenging.

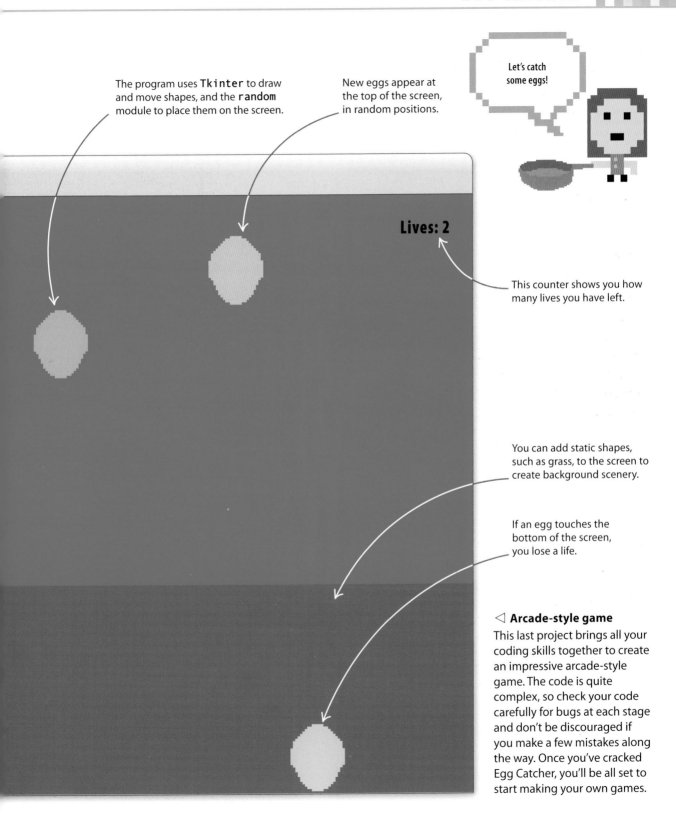

Let's catch some eggs!

The program uses **Tkinter** to draw and move shapes, and the **random** module to place them on the screen.

New eggs appear at the top of the screen, in random positions.

Lives: 2

This counter shows you how many lives you have left.

You can add static shapes, such as grass, to the screen to create background scenery.

If an egg touches the bottom of the screen, you lose a life.

◁ **Arcade-style game**
This last project brings all your coding skills together to create an impressive arcade-style game. The code is quite complex, so check your code carefully for bugs at each stage and don't be discouraged if you make a few mistakes along the way. Once you've cracked Egg Catcher, you'll be all set to start making your own games.

How it works

Once the background is created, the eggs gradually move down the screen, which creates the illusion that they are falling. Using loops, the code continually checks the coordinates of the eggs to see if any have hit the bottom or been caught in the catcher. When an egg is caught or dropped, it is deleted and the program adjusts the score or the number of remaining lives.

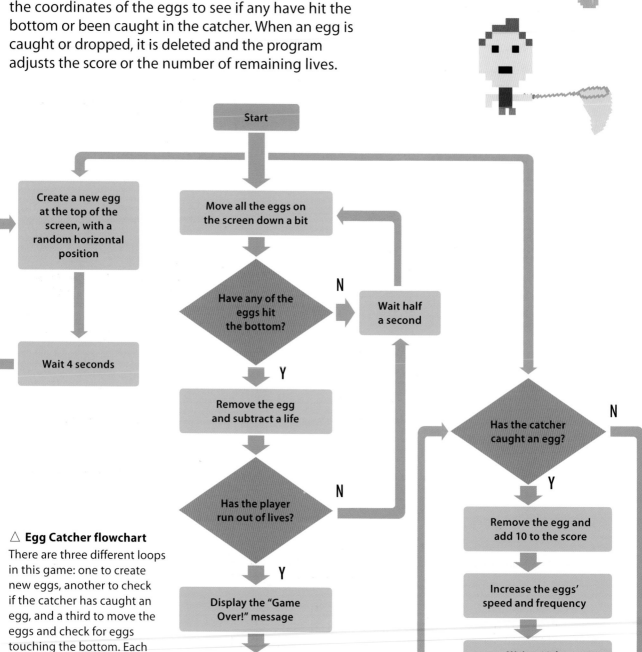

△ **Egg Catcher flowchart**
There are three different loops in this game: one to create new eggs, another to check if the catcher has caught an egg, and a third to move the eggs and check for eggs touching the bottom. Each of the three loops repeats at a different speed.

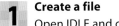

Setting up

First you'll import the parts of Python that you need for this project. Then you'll set things up that so that you're ready to write the main functions for the game.

1 **Create a file**
Open IDLE and create a new file.
Save it as "egg_catcher.py".

2 **Import the modules**
Egg Catcher uses three modules: **itertools** to cycle through some colours; **random** to make the eggs appear in random places; and **Tkinter** to animate the game by creating shapes on the screen. Type these lines at the top of your file.

```
from itertools import cycle
from random import randrange
from tkinter import Canvas, Tk, messagebox, font
```

The code only imports the parts of the modules that you need.

3 **Set up the canvas**
Add this code beneath the import statements. It creates variables for the height and width of the canvas, then uses them to create the canvas itself. To add a bit of scenery to your game, it draws a rectangle to represent some grass and an oval to represent the sun.

This creates the grass.

The **pack()** function tells the program to draw the main window and all its contents.

```
from tkinter import Canvas, Tk, messagebox, font

canvas_width = 800

canvas_height = 400

root = Tk()

c = Canvas(root, width=canvas_width, height=canvas_height, \
background='deep sky blue')

c.create_rectangle(-5, canvas_height - 100, canvas_width + 5, \
canvas_height + 5, fill='sea green', width=0)

c.create_oval(-80, -80, 120, 120, fill='orange', width=0)

c.pack()
```

This creates a window.

The canvas will be sky blue and measure 800 x 400 pixels.

Use a backslash character if you need to split a long line of code over two lines.

This line creates the sun.

4 **See your canvas**
Run the code to see how the canvas looks. You should see a scene with green grass, a blue sky, and a bright sun. If you feel confident, try to make your own scenery with shapes of different colours or sizes. You can always go back to the code above if you run into problems.

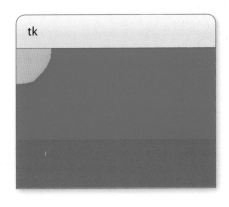

5 Set up the eggs

Now make some variables to store the colours, width, and height of the eggs. You'll also need variables for the score, the speed of the falling eggs, and the interval between new eggs appearing on the screen. The amount they are changed by is determined by the **difficulty_factor** – a lower value for this variable actually makes the game harder.

The **cycle()** function allows you to use each colour in turn.

```
c.pack()

color_cycle = cycle(['light blue', 'light green', 'light pink', 'light yellow', 'light cyan'])
egg_width = 45
egg_height = 55
egg_score = 10
egg_speed = 500
egg_interval = 4000
difficulty_factor = 0.95
```

You score 10 points for catching an egg.

A new egg appears every 4,000 milliseconds (4 seconds).

This is how much the speed and interval change after each catch (closer to 1 is easier).

6 Set up the catcher

Next add the variables for the catcher. As well as variables for its colour and size, there are four variables that store the catcher's starting position. The values for these are calculated using the sizes of the canvas and the catcher. Once these have been calculated, they are used to create the arc that the game uses for the catcher.

Don't forget to save your work.

```
difficulty_factor = 0.95

catcher_color = 'blue'
catcher_width = 100
catcher_height = 100
catcher_start_x = canvas_width / 2 - catcher_width / 2
catcher_start_y = canvas_height - catcher_height - 20
catcher_start_x2 = catcher_start_x + catcher_width
catcher_start_y2 = catcher_start_y + catcher_height

catcher = c.create_arc(catcher_start_x, catcher_start_y, \
                catcher_start_x2, catcher_start_y2, start=200, extent=140, \
                style='arc', outline=catcher_color, width=3)
```

This is the height of the circle that is used to draw the arc.

These lines make the catcher start near the bottom of the canvas, in the centre of the window.

Start drawing at 200 degrees on the circle.

Draw for 140 degrees.

Draw the catcher.

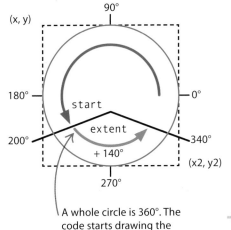

A whole circle is 360°. The code starts drawing the arc just over half way round the circle, at 200°.

◁ How it works

You use an arc to represent the catcher. An arc is one part of a whole circle. **Tkinter** draws circles inside an invisible box. The first two **catcher_start** coordinates (x and y) plot where one corner of the box should be. The second two coordinates (x2 and y2) plot the position of the box's opposite corner. The **create_arc()** function has two parameters, both given in degrees (°), that say where in the circle to draw the arc: **start** says where to start drawing, while **extent** is how many degrees to draw before stopping.

Those pesky birds!

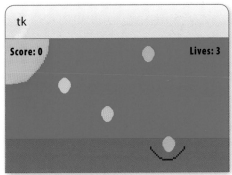

7 Score and lives counters

Add this code under the lines that set up the catcher. It sets the starting score to 0 and creates the text that shows the score on the screen. It also sets the remaining lives to three and displays this number. To check if the code is working, add **root.mainloop()** right at the end and then run the code. Once you've checked, remove this line – you'll add it again later when it's needed.

```python
catcher = c.create_arc(catcher_start_x, catcher_start_y, \
                    catcher_start_x2, catcher_start_y2, start=200, extent=140,
                    style='arc', outline=catcher_color, width=3)

game_font = font.nametofont('TkFixedFont')
game_font.config(size=18)

score = 0
score_text = c.create_text(10, 10, anchor='nw', font=game_font, fill='darkblue', \
                    text='Score: ' + str(score))

lives_remaining = 3
lives_text = c.create_text(canvas_width - 10, 10, anchor='ne', font=game_font, \
                    fill='darkblue', text='Lives ' + str(lives_remaining))
```

This line selects a cool computer-style font.

You can make the text larger or smaller by changing this number.

The player gets three lives.

Falling, scoring, dropping

You've completed all the set-up tasks, so it's time to write the code that runs the game. You'll need functions to create the eggs and make them fall, and some more functions to handle egg catches and egg drops.

8 **Create the eggs**

Add this code. A list keeps track of all the eggs on the screen. The **create_egg()** function decides the coordinates of each new egg (the x coordinate is always randomly selected). Then it creates the egg as an oval and adds it to the list of eggs. Finally, it sets a timer to call the function again after a pause.

```
lives_text = c.create_text(canvas_width - 10, 10, anchor='ne', font=game_font, fill='darkblue', \
                          text='Lives: ' + str(lives_remaining))

eggs = []                              This is a list to keep
                                       track of the eggs.
def create_egg():
    x = randrange(10, 740)             Pick a random position along the top
                                       of the canvas for the new egg.
    y = 40
    new_egg = c.create_oval(x, y, x + egg_width, y + egg_height, fill=next(color_cycle), width=0)
    eggs.append(new_egg)                                                This line of code
    root.after(egg_interval, create_egg)                               creates the oval.
```

The shape is added to the list of eggs.

Call this function again after the number of milliseconds stored in **egg_interval**.

9 **Move the eggs**

After creating the eggs, add the next function, **move_eggs()**, to set them in motion. It loops through the list of all the eggs on screen. For each egg, the y coordinate is increased, which moves the egg down the screen. Once the egg is moved, the program checks whether it has hit the bottom of the screen. If it has, the egg has been dropped and the **egg_dropped()** function is called. Finally, a timer is set to call the **move_eggs()** function again after a short pause.

Help! It's raining eggs!

```
    root.after(egg_interval, create_egg)
                                       Loop through
def move_eggs():                       all the eggs.
    for egg in eggs:
        (egg_x, egg_y, egg_x2, egg_y2) = c.coords(egg)
        c.move(egg, 0, 10)
        if egg_y2 > canvas_height:
            egg_dropped(egg)
    root.after(egg_speed, move_eggs)
```

This line gets each egg's coordinates.

The egg drops down the screen 10 pixels at a time.

Is the egg at the bottom of the screen?

If so, call the function that deals with dropped eggs.

Call this function again after the number of milliseconds stored in **egg_speed**.

10 Oops – egg drop!

Next add the **egg_dropped()** function after **move_eggs()**. When an egg is dropped, it is removed from the list of eggs and then deleted from the canvas. A life is deducted using the **lose_a_life()** function, which you'll create in Step 11. If losing a life means there are no lives left, the "Game Over!" message is shown.

If no lives are left, tell the player that the game is over.

```
root.after(egg_speed, move_eggs)

def egg_dropped(egg):
    eggs.remove(egg)
    c.delete(egg)
    lose_a_life()
    if lives_remaining == 0:
        messagebox.showinfo('Game Over!', 'Final Score: ' \
                            + str(score))
        root.destroy()
```

The egg is removed from the eggs list.

The egg disappears from the canvas.

*This line calls the **lose_a_life()** function.*

The game ends.

11 Lose a life

Losing a life simply involves subtracting a life from the **lives_remaining** variable and then displaying the new value on the screen. Add these lines after the **eggs_dropped()** function.

```
root.destroy()

def lose_a_life():
    global lives_remaining
    lives_remaining -= 1
    c.itemconfigure(lives_text, text='Lives: ' \
                    + str(lives_remaining))
```

This variable needs to be global, as the function will modify it.

The player loses a life.

This line updates the text that shows the remaining lives.

12 Check for a catch

Now add the **check_catch()** function. An egg is caught if it's inside the arc of the catcher. To find out if you've made a catch, the **for** loop gets the coordinates of each egg and compares them with the catcher's coordinates. If there's a match, the egg is caught. Then it's deleted from the list, removed from the screen, and the score is increased.

```
c.itemconfigure(lives_text, text='Lives: ' + str(lives_remaining))

def check_catch():
    (catcher_x, catcher_y, catcher_x2, catcher_y2) = c.coords(catcher)
    for egg in eggs:
        (egg_x, egg_y, egg_x2, egg_y2) = c.coords(egg)
        if catcher_x < egg_x and egg_x2 < catcher_x2 and catcher_y2 - egg_y2 < 40:
            eggs.remove(egg)
            c.delete(egg)
            increase_score(egg_score)
    root.after(100, check_catch)
```

Get the coordinates of the catcher.

Get the coordinates of the eggs.

Increase the score by 10 points.

Is the egg inside the catcher horizontally and vertically?

Call this function again after 100 milliseconds (one-tenth of a second).

13 **Increase the score**

First the score is increased by the value of the **points** parameter. Next the new speed and interval of the eggs are calculated by multiplying their values by the difficulty factor. Finally, the text on the screen is updated with the new score. Add this new function beneath **check_catch()**.

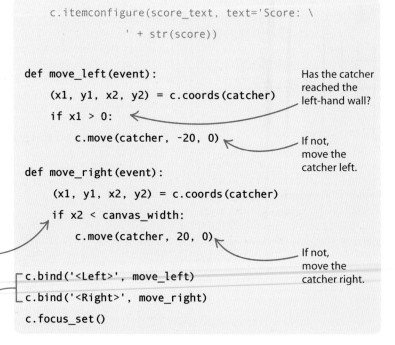

I've caught enough eggs for a nice meal!

```
root.after(100, check_catch)

def increase_score(points):
    global score, egg_speed, egg_interval
    score += points
    egg_speed = int(egg_speed * difficulty_factor)
    egg_interval = int(egg_interval * difficulty_factor)
    c.itemconfigure(score_text, text='Score: ' + str(score))
```

Add to the player's score.

This line updates the text that shows the score.

Catch those eggs!

Now that you've got all the shapes and functions needed for the game, all that's left to add are the controls for the egg catcher and the commands that start the game.

14 **Set up the controls**

The **move_left()** and **move_right()** functions use the coordinates of the catcher to make sure it isn't about to leave the screen. If there's still space to move to, the catcher shifts horizontally by 20 pixels. These two functions are linked to the left and right arrow keys on the keyboard using the **bind()** function. The **focus_set()** function allows the program to detect the key presses. Add the new functions beneath the **increase_score()** function.

```
c.itemconfigure(score_text, text='Score: \
              ' + str(score))

def move_left(event):
    (x1, y1, x2, y2) = c.coords(catcher)
    if x1 > 0:
        c.move(catcher, -20, 0)

def move_right(event):
    (x1, y1, x2, y2) = c.coords(catcher)
    if x2 < canvas_width:
        c.move(catcher, 20, 0)

c.bind('<Left>', move_left)
c.bind('<Right>', move_right)
c.focus_set()
```

Has the catcher reached the left-hand wall?

If not, move the catcher left.

Has the catcher reached the right-hand wall?

These lines call the functions when the keys are pressed.

If not, move the catcher right.

15 Start the game

The three looping functions are started using timers. This ensures they aren't run before the main loop starts. Finally, the `mainloop()` function starts the `Tkinter` loop that manages all your loops and timers. All finished – enjoy the game, and don't let those eggs smash!

```
c.focus_set()

root.after(1000, create_egg)

root.after(1000, move_eggs)

root.after(1000, check_catch)

root.mainloop()
```

The three game loops begin after a slight pause of 1,000 milliseconds (1 second).

This line starts the main `Tkinter` loop.

Hacks and tweaks

To make the game look even better, you can try adding some cool scenery of your own. Fun sounds and music are another great way to make the game more exciting.

◁ **Set the scene**

`Tkinter` allows custom images to be used as backgrounds for a canvas. If your file is a GIF, you can use `tkinter.PhotoImage` to load the file. If your image is a different format, you might want to look into `Pillow` – a helpful image-handling module.

▷ **Make some noise**

To really bring the game to life, add background music or sound effects for catching an egg or losing a life. The module to use for adding sounds is `pygame.mixer`. Remember, **pygame** is not a standard Python module, so you'll need to install it first. You'll also need to have a copy of the sound file you want to play, which you should place in the same folder as your code file. Once that's in place, playing a sound only takes a few lines of code.

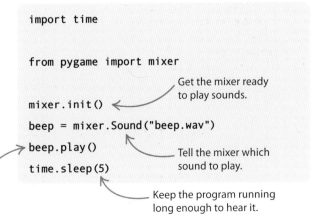

```
import time


from pygame import mixer


mixer.init()

beep = mixer.Sound("beep.wav")

beep.play()

time.sleep(5)
```

Get the mixer ready to play sounds.

Tell the mixer which sound to play.

Play the sound.

Keep the program running long enough to hear it.

Reference

Project reference

Here you'll find the complete Python code for every
project in this book, except for the hacks and tweaks.
If your projects don't run properly, carefully check
your scripts against the code shown here.

Animal Quiz (page 36)

```python
def check_guess(guess, answer):
    global score
    still_guessing = True
    attempt = 0
    while still_guessing and attempt < 3:
        if guess.lower() == answer.lower():
            print('Correct Answer')
            score = score + 1
            still_guessing = False
        else:
            if attempt < 2:
                guess = input('Sorry wrong answer. Try again ')
            attempt = attempt + 1

    if attempt == 3:
        print('The correct answer is ' + answer)

score = 0
print('Guess the Animal')
guess1 = input('Which bear lives at the North Pole? ')
check_guess(guess1, 'polar bear')
guess2 = input('Which is the fastest land animal? ')
check_guess(guess2, 'cheetah')
guess3 = input('Which is the largest animal? ')
check_guess(guess3, 'blue whale')

print('Your score is ' + str(score))
```

Password Picker (page 52)

```python
import random
import string

adjectives = ['sleepy', 'slow', 'smelly',
              'wet', 'fat', 'red',
              'orange', 'yellow', 'green',
              'blue', 'purple', 'fluffy',
```

```
                    'white', 'proud', 'brave']
nouns = ['apple', 'dinosaur', 'ball',
         'toaster', 'goat', 'dragon',
         'hammer', 'duck', 'panda']

print('Welcome to Password Picker!')

while True:
    adjective = random.choice(adjectives)
    noun = random.choice(nouns)
    number = random.randrange(0, 100)
    special_char = random.choice(string.punctuation)

    password = adjective + noun + str(number) + special_char
    print('Your new password is: %s' % password)

    response = input('Would you like another password? Type y or n: ')
    if response == 'n':
        break
```

Nine Lives (page 60)

```
import random

lives = 9
words = ['pizza', 'fairy', 'teeth', 'shirt', 'otter', 'plane']
secret_word = random.choice(words)
clue = list('?????')
heart_symbol = u'\u2764'
guessed_word_correctly = False

def update_clue(guessed_letter, secret_word, clue):
    index = 0
    while index < len(secret_word):
        if guessed_letter == secret_word[index]:
            clue[index] = guessed_letter
        index = index + 1

while lives > 0:
    print(clue)
    print('Lives left: ' + heart_symbol * lives)
    guess = input('Guess a letter or the whole word: ')

    if guess == secret_word:
        guessed_word_correctly = True
        break

    if guess in secret_word:
        update_clue(guess, secret_word, clue)
    else:
```

```
              print('Incorrect. You lose a life')
              lives = lives - 1

if guessed_word_correctly:
    print('You won! The secret word was ' \
+ secret_word)
else:
    print('You lost! The secret word was ' \
+ secret_word)
```

Robot Builder (page 72)

```
import turtle as t

def rectangle(horizontal, vertical, color):
    t.pendown()
    t.pensize(1)
    t.color(color)
    t.begin_fill()
    for counter in range(1, 3):
        t.forward(horizontal)
        t.right(90)
        t.forward(vertical)
        t.right(90)
    t.end_fill()
    t.penup()

t.penup()
t.speed('slow')
t.bgcolor('Dodger blue')

# feet
t.goto(-100, -150)
rectangle(50, 20, 'blue')
t.goto(-30, -150)
rectangle(50, 20, 'blue')

# legs
t.goto(-25, -50)
rectangle(15, 100, 'grey')
t.goto(-55, -50)
rectangle(-15, 100, 'grey')

# body
t.goto(-90, 100)
rectangle(100, 150, 'red')

# arms
t.goto(-150, 70)
rectangle(60, 15, 'grey')
```

```
t.goto(-150, 110)
rectangle(15, 40, 'grey')

t.goto(10, 70)
rectangle(60, 15, 'grey')
t.goto(55, 110)
rectangle(15, 40, 'grey')

# neck
t.goto(-50, 120)
rectangle(15, 20, 'grey')

# head
t.goto(-85, 170)
rectangle(80, 50, 'red')

# eyes
t.goto(-60, 160)
rectangle(30, 10, 'white')
t.goto(-55, 155)
rectangle(5, 5, 'black')
t.goto(-40, 155)
rectangle(5, 5, 'black')

# mouth
t.goto(-65, 135)
rectangle(40, 5, 'black')

t.hideturtle()
```

Kaleido-spiral (page 82)

```
import turtle
from itertools import cycle

colors = cycle(['red', 'orange', 'yellow', \
                'green', 'blue', 'purple'])

def draw_circle(size, angle, shift):
    turtle.pencolor(next(colors))
    turtle.circle(size)
    turtle.right(angle)
    turtle.forward(shift)
    draw_circle(size + 5, angle + 1, shift +
1)

turtle.bgcolor('black')
turtle.speed('fast')
turtle.pensize(4)
draw_circle(30, 0, 1)
```

Starry Night (page 90)

```python
import turtle as t
from random import randint, random

def draw_star(points, size, col, x, y):
    t.penup()
    t.goto(x, y)
    t.pendown
    angle = 180 - (180 / points)
    t.color(col)
    t.begin_fill()
    for i in range(points):
        t.forward(size)
        t.right(angle)
    t.end_fill()

# Main code
t.Screen().bgcolor('dark blue')

while True:
    ranPts = randint(2, 5) * 2 + 1
    ranSize = randint(10, 50)
    ranCol = (random(), random(), random())
    ranX = randint(-350, 300)
    ranY = randint(-250, 250)

    draw_star(ranPts, ranSize, ranCol, ranX, ranY)
```

Mutant Rainbow (page 98)

```python
import random
import turtle as t

def get_line_length():
    choice = input('Enter line length (long, medium, short): ')
    if choice == 'long':
        line_length = 250
    elif choice == 'medium':
        line_length = 200
    else:
        line_length = 100
    return line_length

def get_line_width():
    choice = input('Enter line width (superthick, thick, thin): ')
    if choice == 'superthick':
        line_width = 40
    elif choice == 'thick':
        line_width = 25
```

```
    else:
        line_width = 10
    return line_width

def inside_window():
    left_limit = (-t.window_width() / 2) + 100
    right_limit = (t.window_width() / 2) - 100
    top_limit = (t.window_height() / 2) - 100
    bottom_limit = (-t.window_height() / 2) + 100
    (x, y) = t.pos()
    inside = left_limit < x < right_limit and bottom_limit < y < top_limit
    return inside

def move_turtle(line_length):
    pen_colors = ['red', 'orange', 'yellow', 'green', 'blue', 'purple']
    t.pencolor(random.choice(pen_colors))
    if inside_window():
        angle = random.randint(0, 180)
        t.right(angle)
        t.forward(line_length)
    else:
        t.backward(line_length)

line_length = get_line_length()
line_width = get_line_width()

t.shape('turtle')
t.fillcolor('green')
t.bgcolor('black')
t.speed('fastest')
t.pensize(line_width)

while True:
    move_turtle(line_length)
```

Countdown Calendar (page 110)

```
from tkinter import Tk, Canvas
from datetime import date, datetime

def get_events():
    list_events = []
    with open('events.txt') as file:
        for line in file:
            line = line.rstrip('\n')
            current_event = line.split(',')
            event_date = datetime.strptime(current_event[1], '%d/%m/%y').date()
            current_event[1] = event_date
            list_events.append(current_event)
    return list_events
```

```
def days_between_dates(date1, date2):
    time_between = str(date1 - date2)
    number_of_days = time_between.split(' ')
    return number_of_days[0]

root = Tk()
c = Canvas(root, width=800, height=800, bg='black')
c.pack()
c.create_text(100, 50, anchor='w', fill='orange', font='Arial 28 bold underline', \
              text='My Countdown Calendar')

events = get_events()
today = date.today()

vertical_space = 100

for event in events:
    event_name = event[0]
    days_until = days_between_dates(event[1], today)
    display = 'It is %s days until %s' % (days_until, event_name)
    c.create_text(100, vertical_space, anchor='w', fill='lightblue', \
                  font='Arial 28 bold', text=display)

    vertical_space = vertical_space + 30
```

Ask the Expert (page 120)

```
from tkinter import Tk, simpledialog, messagebox

def read_from_file():
    with open('capital_data.txt') as file:
        for line in file:
            line = line.rstrip('\n')
            country, city = line.split('/')
            the_world[country] = city

def write_to_file(country_name, city_name):
    with open('capital_data.txt', 'a') as file:
        file.write('\n' + country_name + '/' + city_name)

print('Ask the Expert - Capital Cities of the World')
root = Tk()
root.withdraw()
the_world = {}

read_from_file()

while True:
    query_country = simpledialog.askstring('Country', 'Type the name of a country:')

    if query_country in the_world:
```

```
        result = the_world[query_country]
        messagebox.showinfo('Answer',
                            'The capital city of ' + query_country + ' is ' + result + '!')
    else:
        new_city = simpledialog.askstring('Teach me',
                                'I don\'t know! ' +
                                'What is the capital city of ' + query_country + '?')
        the_world[query_country] = new_city
        write_to_file(query_country, new_city)


root.mainloop()
```

Secret Messages (page 130)

```
from tkinter import messagebox, simpledialog, Tk

def is_even(number):
    return number % 2 == 0

def get_even_letters(message):
    even_letters = []
    for counter in range(0, len(message)):
        if is_even(counter):
            even_letters.append(message[counter])
    return even_letters

def get_odd_letters(message):
    odd_letters = []
    for counter in range(0, len(message)):
        if not is_even(counter):
            odd_letters.append(message[counter])
    return odd_letters

def swap_letters(message):
    letter_list = []
    if not is_even(len(message)):
        message = message + 'x'
    even_letters = get_even_letters(message)
    odd_letters = get_odd_letters(message)
    for counter in range(0, int(len(message)/2)):
        letter_list.append(odd_letters[counter])
        letter_list.append(even_letters[counter])
    new_message = ''.join(letter_list)
    return new_message

def get_task():
    task = simpledialog.askstring('Task', 'Do you want to encrypt or decrypt?')
    return task
```

```
def get_message():
    message = simpledialog.askstring('Message', 'Enter the secret message: ')
    return message

root = Tk()

while True:
    task = get_task()
    if task == 'encrypt':
        message = get_message()
        encrypted = swap_letters(message)
        messagebox.showinfo('Ciphertext of the secret message is:', encrypted)
    elif task == 'decrypt':
        message = get_message()
        decrypted = swap_letters(message)
        messagebox.showinfo('Plaintext of the secret message is:', decrypted)
    else:
        break
root.mainloop()
```

Screen Pet (page 142)

```
from tkinter import HIDDEN, NORMAL, Tk, Canvas

def toggle_eyes():
    current_color = c.itemcget(eye_left, 'fill')
    new_color = c.body_color if current_color == 'white' else 'white'
    current_state = c.itemcget(pupil_left, 'state')
    new_state = NORMAL if current_state == HIDDEN else HIDDEN
    c.itemconfigure(pupil_left, state=new_state)
    c.itemconfigure(pupil_right, state=new_state)
    c.itemconfigure(eye_left, fill=new_color)
    c.itemconfigure(eye_right, fill=new_color)

def blink():
    toggle_eyes()
    root.after(250, toggle_eyes)
    root.after(3000, blink)

def toggle_pupils():
    if not c.eyes_crossed:
        c.move(pupil_left, 10, -5)
        c.move(pupil_right, -10, -5)
        c.eyes_crossed = True
    else:
        c.move(pupil_left, -10, 5)
        c.move(pupil_right, 10, 5)
        c.eyes_crossed = False
```

```
def toggle_tongue():
    if not c.tongue_out:
        c.itemconfigure(tongue_tip, state=NORMAL)
        c.itemconfigure(tongue_main, state=NORMAL)
        c.tongue_out = True
    else:
        c.itemconfigure(tongue_tip, state=HIDDEN)
        c.itemconfigure(tongue_main, state=HIDDEN)
        c.tongue_out = False

def cheeky(event):
    toggle_tongue()
    toggle_pupils()
    hide_happy(event)
    root.after(1000, toggle_tongue)
    root.after(1000, toggle_pupils)
    return

def show_happy(event):
    if (20 <= event.x and event.x <= 350) and (20 <= event.y and event.y <= 350):
        c.itemconfigure(cheek_left, state=NORMAL)
        c.itemconfigure(cheek_right, state=NORMAL)
        c.itemconfigure(mouth_happy, state=NORMAL)
        c.itemconfigure(mouth_normal, state=HIDDEN)
        c.itemconfigure(mouth_sad, state=HIDDEN)
        c.happy_level = 10
    return

def hide_happy(event):
    c.itemconfigure(cheek_left, state=HIDDEN)
    c.itemconfigure(cheek_right, state=HIDDEN)
    c.itemconfigure(mouth_happy, state=HIDDEN)
    c.itemconfigure(mouth_normal, state=NORMAL)
    c.itemconfigure(mouth_sad, state=HIDDEN)
    return

def sad():
    if c.happy_level == 0:
        c.itemconfigure(mouth_happy, state=HIDDEN)
        c.itemconfigure(mouth_normal, state=HIDDEN)
        c.itemconfigure(mouth_sad, state=NORMAL)
    else:
        c.happy_level -= 1
    root.after(5000, sad)

root = Tk()
c = Canvas(root, width=400, height=400)
c.configure(bg='dark blue', highlightthickness=0)
c.body_color = 'SkyBlue1'
```

```
body = c.create_oval(35, 20, 365, 350, outline=c.body_color, fill=c.body_color)
ear_left = c.create_polygon(75, 80, 75, 10, 165, 70, outline=c.body_color, fill=c.body_color)
ear_right = c.create_polygon(255, 45, 325, 10, 320, 70, outline=c.body_color, fill=c.body_color)
foot_left = c.create_oval(65, 320, 145, 360, outline=c.body_color, fill=c.body_color)
foot_right = c.create_oval(250, 320, 330, 360, outline=c.body_color, fill=c.body_color)

eye_left = c.create_oval(130, 110, 160, 170, outline='black', fill='white')
pupil_left = c.create_oval(140, 145, 150, 155, outline='black', fill='black')
eye_right = c.create_oval(230, 110, 260, 170, outline='black', fill='white')
pupil_right = c.create_oval(240, 145, 250, 155, outline='black', fill='black')

mouth_normal = c.create_line(170, 250, 200, 272, 230, 250, smooth=1, width=2, state=NORMAL)
mouth_happy = c.create_line(170, 250, 200, 282, 230, 250, smooth=1, width=2, state=HIDDEN)
mouth_sad = c.create_line(170, 250, 200, 232, 230, 250, smooth=1, width=2, state=HIDDEN)
tongue_main = c.create_rectangle(170, 250, 230, 290, outline='red', fill='red', state=HIDDEN)
tongue_tip = c.create_oval(170, 285, 230, 300, outline='red', fill='red', state=HIDDEN)

cheek_left = c.create_oval(70, 180, 120, 230, outline='pink', fill='pink', state=HIDDEN)
cheek_right = c.create_oval(280, 180, 330, 230, outline='pink', fill='pink', state=HIDDEN)

c.pack()

c.bind('<Motion>', show_happy)
c.bind('<Leave>', hide_happy)
c.bind('<Double-1>', cheeky)

c.happy_level = 10
c.eyes_crossed = False
c.tongue_out = False

root.after(1000, blink)
root.after(5000, sad)
root.mainloop()
```

Caterpillar (page 158)

```
import random
import turtle as t

t.bgcolor('yellow')

caterpillar = t.Turtle()
caterpillar.shape('square')
caterpillar.color('red')
caterpillar.speed(0)
caterpillar.penup()
caterpillar.hideturtle()

leaf = t.Turtle()
```

```
leaf_shape = ((0, 0), (14, 2), (18, 6), (20, 20), (6, 18), (2, 14))
t.register_shape('leaf', leaf_shape)
leaf.shape('leaf')
leaf.color('green')
leaf.penup()
leaf.hideturtle()
leaf.speed(0)

game_started = False
text_turtle = t.Turtle()
text_turtle.write('Press SPACE to start', align='center', font=('Arial', 16, 'bold'))
text_turtle.hideturtle()

score_turtle = t.Turtle()
score_turtle.hideturtle()
score_turtle.speed(0)

def outside_window():
    left_wall = -t.window_width() / 2
    right_wall = t.window_width() / 2
    top_wall = t.window_height() / 2
    bottom_wall = -t.window_height() / 2
    (x, y) = caterpillar.pos()
    outside = \
            x< left_wall or \
            x> right_wall or \
            y< bottom_wall or \
            y> top_wall
    return outside

def game_over():
    caterpillar.color('yellow')
    leaf.color('yellow')
    t.penup()
    t.hideturtle()
    t.write('GAME OVER!', align='center', font=('Arial', 30, 'normal'))

def display_score(current_score):
    score_turtle.clear()
    score_turtle.penup()
    x = (t.window_width() / 2) - 50
    y = (t.window_height() / 2) - 50
    score_turtle.setpos(x, y)
    score_turtle.write(str(current_score), align='right', font=('Arial', 40, 'bold'))

def place_leaf():
    leaf.ht()
    leaf.setx(random.randint(-200, 200))
```

```
        leaf.sety(random.randint(-200, 200))
        leaf.st()

def start_game():
    global game_started
    if game_started:
        return
    game_started = True

    score = 0
    text_turtle.clear()

    caterpillar_speed = 2
    caterpillar_length = 3
    caterpillar.shapesize(1, caterpillar_length, 1)
    caterpillar.showturtle()
    display_score(score)
    place_leaf()

    while True:
        caterpillar.forward(caterpillar_speed)
        if caterpillar.distance(leaf) < 20:
            place_leaf()
            caterpillar_length = caterpillar_length + 1
            caterpillar.shapesize(1, caterpillar_length, 1)
            caterpillar_speed = caterpillar_speed + 1
            score = score + 10
            display_score(score)
        if outside_window():
            game_over()
            break

def move_up():
    if caterpillar.heading() == 0 or caterpillar.heading() == 180:
        caterpillar.setheading(90)

def move_down():
    if caterpillar.heading() == 0 or caterpillar.heading() == 180:
        caterpillar.setheading(270)

def move_left():
    if caterpillar.heading() == 90 or caterpillar.heading() == 270:
        caterpillar.setheading(180)

def move_right():
    if caterpillar.heading() == 90 or caterpillar.heading() == 270:
        caterpillar.setheading(0)
t.onkey(start_game, 'space')
t.onkey(move_up, 'Up')
t.onkey(move_right, 'Right')
```

```
t.onkey(move_down, 'Down')
t.onkey(move_left, 'Left')
t.listen()
t.mainloop()
```

Snap (page 168)

```
import random
import time
from tkinter import Tk, Canvas, HIDDEN, NORMAL

def next_shape():
    global shape
    global previous_color
    global current_color

    previous_color = current_color

    c.delete(shape)
    if len(shapes) > 0:
        shape = shapes.pop()
        c.itemconfigure(shape, state=NORMAL)
        current_color = c.itemcget(shape, 'fill')
        root.after(1000, next_shape)
    else:
        c.unbind('q')
        c.unbind('p')
        if player1_score > player2_score:
            c.create_text(200, 200, text='Winner: Player 1')
        elif player2_score > player1_score:
            c.create_text(200, 200, text='Winner: Player 2')
        else:
            c.create_text(200, 200, text='Draw')
        c.pack()

def snap(event):
    global shape
    global player1_score
    global player2_score
    valid = False

    c.delete(shape)
    if previous_color == current_color:
        valid = True

    if valid:
        if event.char == 'q':
            player1_score = player1_score + 1
        else:
```

```
                player2_score = player2_score + 1
            shape = c.create_text(200, 200, text='SNAP! You score 1 point!')
        else:
            if event.char == 'q':
                player1_score = player1_score - 1
            else:
                player2_score = player2_score - 1
            shape = c.create_text(200, 200, text='WRONG! You lose 1 point!')
        c.pack()
        root.update_idletasks()
        time.sleep(1)

root = Tk()
root.title('Snap')
c = Canvas(root, width=400, height=400)

shapes = []

circle = c.create_oval(35, 20, 365, 350, outline='black', fill='black', state=HIDDEN)
shapes.append(circle)
circle = c.create_oval(35, 20, 365, 350, outline='red', fill='red', state=HIDDEN)
shapes.append(circle)
circle = c.create_oval(35, 20, 365, 350, outline='green', fill='green', state=HIDDEN)
shapes.append(circle)
circle = c.create_oval(35, 20, 365, 350, outline='blue', fill='blue', state=HIDDEN)
shapes.append(circle)

rectangle = c.create_rectangle(35, 100, 365, 270, outline='black', fill='black', state=HIDDEN)
shapes.append(rectangle)
rectangle = c.create_rectangle(35, 100, 365, 270, outline='red', fill='red', state=HIDDEN)
shapes.append(rectangle)
rectangle = c.create_rectangle(35, 100, 365, 270, outline='green', fill='green', state=HIDDEN)
shapes.append(rectangle)
rectangle = c.create_rectangle(35, 100, 365, 270, outline='blue', fill='blue', state=HIDDEN)
shapes.append(rectangle)

square = c.create_rectangle(35, 20, 365, 350, outline='black', fill='black', state=HIDDEN)
shapes.append(square)
square = c.create_rectangle(35, 20, 365, 350, outline='red', fill='red', state=HIDDEN)
shapes.append(square)
square = c.create_rectangle(35, 20, 365, 350, outline='green', fill='green', state=HIDDEN)
shapes.append(square)
square = c.create_rectangle(35, 20, 365, 350, outline='blue', fill='blue', state=HIDDEN)
shapes.append(square)
c.pack()

random.shuffle(shapes)

shape = None
```

```
previous_color = ''
current_color = ''
player1_score = 0
player2_score = 0

root.after(3000, next_shape)
c.bind('q', snap)
c.bind('p', snap)
c.focus_set()

root.mainloop()
```

Matchmaker (page 180)

```
import random
import time
from tkinter import Tk, Button, DISABLED

def show_symbol(x, y):
    global first
    global previousX, previousY
    buttons[x, y]['text'] = button_symbols[x, y]
    buttons[x, y].update_idletasks()

    if first:
        previousX = x
        previousY = y
        first = False
    elif previousX != x or previousY != y:
        if buttons[previousX, previousY]['text'] != buttons[x, y]['text']:
            time.sleep(0.5)
            buttons[previousX, previousY]['text'] = ''
            buttons[x, y]['text'] = ''
        else:
            buttons[previousX, previousY]['command'] = DISABLED
            buttons[x, y]['command'] = DISABLED
        first = True

root = Tk()
root.title('Matchmaker')
root.resizable(width=False, height=False)
buttons = {}
first = True
previousX = 0
previousY = 0
button_symbols = {}
symbols = [u'\u2702', u'\u2702', u'\u2705', u'\u2705', u'\u2708', u'\u2708',
           u'\u2709', u'\u2709', u'\u270A', u'\u270A', u'\u270B', u'\u270B',
```

```
            u'\u270C', u'\u270C', u'\u270F', u'\u270F', u'\u2712', u'\u2712',
            u'\u2714', u'\u2714', u'\u2716', u'\u2716', u'\u2728', u'\u2728']
random.shuffle(symbols)

for x in range(6):
    for y in range(4):
        button = Button(command=lambda x=x, y=y: show_symbol(x, y), width=3, height=3)
        button.grid(column=x, row=y)
        buttons[x, y] = button
        button_symbols[x, y] = symbols.pop()

root.mainloop()
```

Egg Catcher (page 190)

```
from itertools import cycle
from random import randrange
from tkinter import Canvas, Tk, messagebox, font

canvas_width = 800
canvas_height = 400

root = Tk()
c = Canvas(root, width=canvas_width, height=canvas_height, background='deep sky blue')
c.create_rectangle(-5, canvas_height - 100, canvas_width + 5, canvas_height + 5, \
                   fill='sea green', width=0)
c.create_oval(-80, -80, 120, 120, fill='orange', width=0)
c.pack()

color_cycle = cycle(['light blue', 'light green', 'light pink', 'light yellow', 'light cyan'])
egg_width = 45
egg_height = 55
egg_score = 10
egg_speed = 500
egg_interval = 4000
difficulty_factor = 0.95

catcher_color = 'blue'
catcher_width = 100
catcher_height = 100
catcher_start_x = canvas_width / 2 - catcher_width / 2
catcher_start_y = canvas_height - catcher_height - 20
catcher_start_x2 = catcher_start_x + catcher_width
catcher_start_y2 = catcher_start_y + catcher_height

catcher = c.create_arc(catcher_start_x, catcher_start_y, \
                       catcher_start_x2, catcher_start_y2, start=200, extent=140, \
                       style='arc', outline=catcher_color, width=3)
```

```
game_font = font.nametofont('TkFixedFont')
game_font.config(size=18)

score = 0
score_text = c.create_text(10, 10, anchor='nw', font=game_font, fill='darkblue', \
                           text='Score: ' + str(score))

lives_remaining = 3
lives_text = c.create_text(canvas_width - 10, 10, anchor='ne', font=game_font, fill='darkblue', \
                           text='Lives: ' + str(lives_remaining))

eggs = []

def create_egg():
    x = randrange(10, 740)
    y = 40
    new_egg = c.create_oval(x, y, x + egg_width, y + egg_height, fill=next(color_cycle), width=0)
    eggs.append(new_egg)
    root.after(egg_interval, create_egg)

def move_eggs():
    for egg in eggs:
        (egg_x, egg_y, egg_x2, egg_y2) = c.coords(egg)
        c.move(egg, 0, 10)
        if egg_y2 > canvas_height:
            egg_dropped(egg)
    root.after(egg_speed, move_eggs)

def egg_dropped(egg):
    eggs.remove(egg)
    c.delete(egg)
    lose_a_life()
    if lives_remaining == 0:
        messagebox.showinfo('Game Over!', 'Final Score: ' + str(score))
        root.destroy()

def lose_a_life():
    global lives_remaining
    lives_remaining -= 1
    c.itemconfigure(lives_text, text='Lives: ' + str(lives_remaining))

def check_catch():
    (catcher_x, catcher_y, catcher_x2, catcher_y2) = c.coords(catcher)
    for egg in eggs:
        (egg_x, egg_y, egg_x2, egg_y2) = c.coords(egg)
        if catcher_x < egg_x and egg_x2 < catcher_x2 and catcher_y2 - egg_y2 < 40:
            eggs.remove(egg)
            c.delete(egg)
            increase_score(egg_score)
```

```
        root.after(100, check_catch)

def increase_score(points):
    global score, egg_speed, egg_interval
    score += points
    egg_speed = int(egg_speed * difficulty_factor)
    egg_interval = int(egg_interval * difficulty_factor)
    c.itemconfigure(score_text, text='Score: ' + str(score))

def move_left(event):
    (x1, y1, x2, y2) = c.coords(catcher)
    if x1 > 0:
        c.move(catcher, -20, 0)

def move_right(event):
    (x1, y1, x2, y2) = c.coords(catcher)
    if x2 < canvas_width:
        c.move(catcher, 20, 0)

c.bind('<Left>', move_left)
c.bind('<Right>', move_right)
c.focus_set()

root.after(1000, create_egg)
root.after(1000, move_eggs)
root.after(1000, check_catch)
root.mainloop()
```

Glossary

ASCII
"American Standard Code for Information Interchange" – a code used for storing text characters as binary code.

Boolean expression
A statement that is either true or false, leading to two possible outcomes.

branch
A point in a program where two different options are available to choose from.

bug
An error in a program's code that makes it behave in an unexpected way.

call
To use a function in a program.

comment
A text note added by a programmer to a program that makes the code easier to understand and is ignored by the program when it runs.

condition
A "true or false" statement used to make a decision in a program. See also *Boolean expression*.

constant
A fixed value that can't be changed.

coordinates
A pair of numbers that pinpoint an exact location. Usually written as (x, y).

data
Information, such as text, symbols, and numerical values.

dictionary
A collection of data items stored in pairs, such as countries and their capital cities.

debug
To look for and correct errors in a program.

encryption
A way of encoding data so that only certain people can read or access it.

event
Something a computer program can react to, such as a key being pressed or the mouse being clicked.

file
A collection of data stored with a name.

flag variable
A variable that can have two states, such as true and false.

float
A number with a decimal point in it.

flowchart
A diagram that shows a program as a sequence of steps and decisions.

function
Code that carries out a specific task, working like a program within a program. Also called a procedure, subprogram, or subroutine.

global variable
A variable that works throughout every part of a program. See also *local variable*.

graphics
Visual elements on a screen that are not text, such as pictures, icons, and symbols.

GUI
The GUI, or graphical user interface, is the name for the buttons and windows that make up the part of the program you can see and interact with.

hack
An ingenious change to code that makes it do something new or simplifies it. (Also, accessing a computer without permission.)

hacker
A person who breaks into a computer system. "White hat" hackers work for computer security companies and look for problems in order to fix them. "Black hat" hackers break into computer systems to cause harm or to make profit from them.

indent
When a block of code is placed further to the right than the previous block. An indent is usually four spaces. Every line in a particular block of code must be indented by the same amount.

index number
A number given to an item in a list. In Python, the index number of the first item will be 0, the second item 1, and so on.

input
Data that is entered into a computer. Keyboards, mice, and microphones can be used to input data.

integer
A whole number. An integer does not contain a decimal point and is not written as a fraction.

interface
The means by which the user interacts with software or hardware. See *GUI*.

library
A collection of functions that can be reused in other projects.

list
A collection of items stored in numbered order.

local variable
A variable that works only within a limited part of a program, such as a function. See also *global variable*.

loop
A part of a program that repeats itself, removing the need to type out the same piece of code multiple times.

module
A package of ready-made code that can be imported into a Python program, making lots of useful functions available.

nested loop
A loop inside another loop.

operating system (OS)
The program that controls everything on a computer, such as Windows, macOS, or Linux.

operator
A symbol that performs a specific function: for example, "+" (addition) or "−" (subtraction).

output
Data that is produced by a computer program and viewed by the user.

parameter
A value given to a function. The value of a parameter is assigned by the line of code that calls the function.

pixels
Tiny dots that make up a digital image.

program
A set of instructions that a computer follows in order to complete a task.

programming language
A language that is used to give instructions to a computer.

Python
A popular programming language created by Guido van Rossum. It is a great language for beginners to learn.

random
A function in a computer program that allows unpredictable outcomes. Useful when creating games.

recursion
Creating a loop by telling a function to call itself.

return value
The variable or data that is passed back after a function has been called (run).

run
The command to make a program start.

software
Programs that run on a computer and control how it works.

statement
The smallest complete instruction a programming language can be broken down into.

string
A series of characters. Strings can contain numbers, letters, or symbols, such as a colon.

syntax
The rules that determine how code must be written in order for it to work properly.

toggle
To switch between two different settings.

tuple
A list of items separated by commas and surrounded by brackets. Tuples are similar to lists, except you can't change them after they've been created.

turtle graphics
A Python module that lets you draw shapes by moving a robotic turtle across the screen.

Unicode
A universal code used by computers to represent thousands of symbols and text characters.

variable
A place to store data that can change in a program, such as the player's score. A variable has a name and a value.

widget
A part of a Tkinter GUI (graphical user interface) that performs a specific function, such as a button or menu.

Index

Page numbers in **bold** refer to main entries.

Acknowledgments

Dorling Kindersley would like to thank Caroline Hunt for proofreading;
Jonathan Burd for the index; Tina Jindal and Sonia Yooshing for editorial
assistance; Deeksha Saikia, Priyanjali Narain, and Arpita Dasgupta for
code testing.